SAVED TO REMEMBER

SAVED TO REMEMBER

RAOUL WALLENBERG, BUDAPEST 1944 AND AFTER

FRANK VAJDA

© Copyright 2016 Frank Vajda
All rights reserved. Apart from any uses permitted by Australia's Copyright Act 1968, no part of this book may be reproduced by any process without prior written permission from the copyright owners. Inquiries should be directed to the publisher.

Monash University Publishing
Matheson Library and Information Services Building
40 Exhibition Walk
Monash University
Clayton, Victoria 3800, Australia
www.publishing.monash.edu

Monash University Publishing brings to the world publications which advance the best traditions of humane and enlightened thought.

Monash University Publishing titles pass through a rigorous process of independent peer review.

www.publishing.monash.edu/books/sr-9781925377088.html

Series: Biography

Design: Les Thomas

Cover images:
Front cover, top: Frank Vajda as a young child. From the Vajda family collection.
Front cover, bottom: The Pest bridgehead of the destroyed Erzsébet Bridge as seen from across the Danube. Photograph by Dr. István Kramer.
Back cover: Raoul Wallenberg, Photograph Vertical File. From the Bentley Historical Library.

National Library of Australia Cataloguing-in-Publication entry:

Creator:	Vajda, F. J. E. (Frank J. E.), author.
Title:	Saved to remember : Raoul Wallenberg, Budapest 1944 and after / Frank Vajda.
ISBN:	9781925377088 (paperback)
Subjects:	Vajda, F. J. E. (Frank J. E.)
	Wallenberg, Raoul, 1912-1947.
	Jews--Hungary--History--20th century.
	Holocaust, Jewish (1939-1945)--Hungary.
	Holocaust survivors--Hungary.
	Hungary--History--1918-1945.
Dewey Number:	940.5318092

Printed in Australia by Griffin Press an Accredited ISO AS/NZS 14001:2004 Environmental Management System printer.

The paper this book is printed on is certified against the Forest Stewardship Council ® Standards. Griffin Press holds FSC chain of custody certification SGS-COC-005088. FSC promotes environmentally responsible, socially beneficial and economically viable management of the world's forests.

CONTENTS

Acknowledgments..vi
Dedication..viii
Introduction...ix

PART ONE: JUST A SURVIVOR

Chapter One	Early Recollections of My Family.............	13
Chapter Two	The Plight of Hungarian Jewry...............	18
Chapter Three	Eight Close Shaves........................	26
Chapter Four	My Parents	36
Chapter Five	The Fate of My Father.....................	48
Chapter Six	Four Related Families.....................	56
Chapter Seven	The Fate of Others........................	71
Chapter Eight	Post-war Hungary.........................	78
Chapter Nine	A New Life in Australia	89
Chapter Ten	My Later Medical Career	101

PART TWO: RAOUL WALLENBERG ... AS I REMEMBER

Chapter Eleven	Raoul Wallenberg in Hungary	109
Chapter Twelve	The Soviet Connection	121
Chapter Thirteen	Archbishop Verolino, One of the Righteous....	130
Chapter Fourteen	Wallenberg's Honorary Australian Citizenship ..	136

Reflections..147
Appendix One: Depositions 148
Appendix Two: Free Wallenberg Letter, c. 1984 157
Appendix Three: Per Anger Letter, 1999 158
About the Author 160

ACKNOWLEDGMENTS

I owe an immense debt to many people, who helped to get this modest book to fruition. I wish to thank first of all my parents and family who have provided the material for this book, and many friends and colleagues who have encouraged me to proceed with publication.

The historical sections are an overview of my experiences as a survivor and a keen student of the period, with a focus on events in my early life. Although I started a course in History at Melbourne University after graduating in Medicine, I opted for taking on higher studies in science, but have kept up my review of the historical events. I am immensely grateful to Mrs Nina Lagergren for her support, friendship and encouragement over thirty-five years, and providing historical details, glimpses and documents about her brother, Raoul Wallenberg. The late Ambassador Per Anger had been a wonderful friend and collaborator in all matters related to the Swedish Mission in 1944.

Sonja Sonnenfeld was a constant source of energy and initiatives aimed at Raoul's attempted rescue and of information received worldwide. I am grateful to the late Sir Zelman Cowen, Patron of the Australian Free Wallenberg Committee, the late Senator Don Chipp for embracing the Wallenberg cause thirty-four years ago, Jill O'Brien, former Mayor of Kew, and Dr John Copland, who served as Secretary of the Wallenberg Committee for many years.

I wish to thank Sponsors of the Wallenberg Committee, the giants of the Australian political and cultural scene, including R. J. L Hawke, Sir Douglas Wright, Stephen Murray-Smith, Thomas Keneally, Phillip Adams, Max Harris, C. M. H Clark, Gareth Evans, Mina Fink, Malcolm Fraser, Walter Jona, Barry Jones, Leonie Kramer, John Levi, Andrew Peacock, David Penman, Morris L. West and David Williamson.

I am grateful to Josh Frydenberg and Mark Dreyfus for raising the issue of Wallenberg in Parliament, and to Julia Gillard's government for enabling the granting of honorary citizenship to Wallenberg, with full support of the Opposition led by Tony Abbott. I am deeply indebted to Senator Bob Carr for exerting his influence, prestige and knowledge to streamline the road to the honorary citizenship. His contribution is acknowledged also in the correspondence included in the book.

Acknowledgments

In preparing this book Patrick Morgan helped me with editorial guidance and my son Simon Raoul contributed to computer related matters and their solution. I wish to thank them sincerely. I discussed individual sections with colleagues and participants in many events, and received much helpful advice, from H. Glasbeek, Count Gabriel Carr, P. Farago, J. Wilder, P. Barta, E. Byrne, M. Eadie, S. Davis, D. Horgan, R. Hjorth, J. King E. Perucca, P. Perucca, H. Corbett, P. Bladin, R. Baker, S. Berkovic, S. Davis, O. White and B. Jangfeldt. Others offering suggestions and advice includeed J. Anger, J. Frydenberg, J. Schiff, the late Jacob Rosenberg – poet, friend and historian – J. Dammery, M. Jubb, D. de Lacey, T. O'Brien, G. Donnan, A. Sempill, G. Quail, K. and N. Wacz, W. Hyde, R. J. O'Bryan, T. J. Martin, M. Newton, R. Moore, Richard Divall, Maestro of the Australian music world, and many other friends too numerous to mention individually. I thank them very much for their support.

The original draft was typed by Y. Dunstan and photographs were provided by relatives of participants mentioned. Interest was kindled by many colleagues and patients, and friends J. Caulfield, P. and C. Morris, A. Roten and N. Buchanan. I wish to thank my wife Michele for tolerating the endless discussions on topics related to this book, and finally I am much indebted to my editor, Dr Nathan Hollier, Director of Monash University Publishing, for his instant interest in having this book considered for publication, his encouraging comments and helpful suggestions regarding changes and improvements. I wish to acknowledge the splendid support, skill and expertise of Leslie Thomas, Sarah Cannon, and Jo Mullins of Monash University Publishing.

Photographs from the Ambassador Ceremony and the Honorary Citizenship certificate were provided by Emilio Perucca and Jan Anger and used with their permission. Photos of colleagues and family were provided with their permission. Documents obtained over fifty years ago were issued by services no longer in existence, such as the Committee for Deportees.

F. Vajda, Melbourne 2016

DEDICATION

*This book is dedicated to the memory of
my beloved parents, László Vajda,
murdered by the Germans in Mauthausen,
Mária Vajda, to whom I owe everything,
and Raoul Wallenberg, Hero of the Holocaust.*

INTRODUCTION

In December 1950 my mother took me by train to Ebensee in Salzkammergut in the Austrian mountains. Picturesque scenery surrounds the whole region, yet it was no ordinary excursion. She wanted me to see the former concentration camp, KZ Lager Ebensee, Kommando Mauthausen, where in March 1945 the Nazis murdered my father by starving him to death. On this journey, which took about six hours from Steyr, she told me the story of how by accident she met a man who was a companion of my father from the time he disappeared to become a victim of the Shoah. I recount that story later in the book.

An inscription on the large memorial stone in the KZ cemetery was clearly visible in the centre of a field, dotted with stones, stars of David, and small plaques denoting the sites of mass graves and individual memorials, placed more by conjecture than based on actual knowledge of where the mourners thought their beloved lay buried, or their ashes were placed after cremation. The text on the main stone memorial was inscribed in four languages. I stared at it for a long time and then copied down the English version. It reads as follows:

> Here are resting in peace the political prisoners murdered in the years 1943–1945 in the Hitler concentration camps at Ebensee. They were Poles, Frenchmen, Jews, Czechs, Yugoslavs, Russians, Italians, Belgians, Dutchmen, Spaniards and Austrians.
>
> For the eternal memory of the murdered defenders of freedom and for the everlasting infamy of the German nation, this monument was erected by Poles, former political prisoners of German concentration camps at Ebensee.

Looking at that inscription for a long time, I sifted the earth in my hand and went on to read the individual plaques over some of the graves. Quietly, sadly and with clenched teeth I said to myself: I shall not forget.

I was 14 years old.

This story is not about the Holocaust in its entirety, but rather about responses to events that happened to me. It is also my explanation of how I cope and respond to other survivors and to the rest of mankind in the wake of an event which in magnitude and horror has probably eclipsed most others in recorded history.

I survived by a series of near misses and coincidences. Although not mutilated physically, I became scarred emotionally as a result. Being able to recollect in writing these events and their effect on conditioning my subsequent responses is an opportunity I am grateful for. This book also includes my reflections on these events. Almost certainly my views are not unique; they are held by many people who find it difficult to express them, certainly openly, or to reconcile them with views generally accepted by writers concerned with the Holocaust.

This book relates my life from my earliest recollections of our extended Jewish family in Budapest to the present day. This narrative however is secondary to my prime motive of expressing feelings of sorrow and shame, and, as much as any single person can, trying to prevent the recurrence of circumstances that culminate in racial mass murder. The underlying impulse to write has been present for many years, but professional responsibilities over the past forty years intruded on my time, leaving me little time to write about matters not connected with medicine.

A notable exception is the Raoul Wallenberg case, which has been a recurrent interest. In the 1980s the recurrence of the world's interest in Raoul Wallenberg made me resolve to devote my energies to his rescue or, if he were not still alive, to get his name recognised as a hero. Involvement in this saga, coupled with an increasingly deep commitment in medical research, enabled me to combine these two leitmotifs and eventually establish the Wallenberg Centre of Clinical Neuropharmacology at St. Vincent's Hospital in Melbourne. I fervently hope the Centre will honour Raoul Wallenberg, to whom I believe I and many others owe our lives.

An opportunity during a sabbatical period started me writing. The immediate impulse was provided by Bruno Bettelheim's book *Surviving and Other Essays*. His passionate and succinctly expressed views aroused in me a feeling of enthusiasm, giving me the impetus to write. One aspect of his book however was less than satisfying. He did not go on to describe how the survivors and their descendants behaved after being liberated from their catastrophic experiences. How did they react to events which made all other subsequent ones appear trivial in comparison? I was curious to learn what survivors and their circle of friends, both Jewish and gentile, have learnt from their days of horror during the Second World War, and how they try to prevent a repetition of them.

Have they learnt to abandon the external trappings which led to their environment, or to react more favourably to their shortcomings? Or has the Holocaust – like many other lessons from history – been repressed, its conclusions never articulated and its lessons allowed to go unheeded? After the First World War, the democracies, exhausted by the slaughter, relaxed their guard, and Nazi aggression was allowed to rise, become overwhelming and lead to catastrophe. Is it reasonable to expect the Jewish people to be much different now or wiser, or to do anything to heed the fate of the six million? In discussing these questions with a gentile friend, he looked surprised and said: 'You can see the views of both sides, those of the persecuted and also the bystanders.' His comment gave me the final impetus to write.

From the perspective of more than seventy years of age, it is now possible to complete my autobiography, first started many years ago. I must class myself a late maturer, or perhaps someone who has not lost his childhood. This childhood was to haunt me forever, but I never considered myself unhappy with what I was given at the start, grieving though I had been for the loss of parents, family, home and friends as a result of the Jewish tragedy known as the Holocaust. I have gained many wonderful new friends and have a loving family, so that in the overall balance my life has been very much a fulfilling one, and one can only speculate on what might have been if Hitler had never existed.

This story is an untidy mixture of events, people, anecdotes and a rather simple philosophy. Though my observations have been tempered by a defensive attitude forged in a disfigured childhood, I hope they are representative and not just trivial. When I once told somebody I was writing my autobiography, she asked me what it was about. I said I was a victim of the Holocaust, and she abruptly remarked 'Just another survivor'. I am proud to be just another survivor. In 2003 when I was awarded a major Swedish decoration, the Swedish Star, no-one would have been more surprised than I was. The reward was unexpected, and I felt shaken rather than elated. From the yellow Jewish star to the Polar Star has been a long journey, and maybe will interest those who knew some parts of it but not the whole story.

The birth of our son, who bears Raoul's name as well those of Simon Wiesenthal and of my martyred Father, testifies to my commitment to the memory of those people, and to my resolve to fight racism. My wife Michele has given unstinting support in these endeavours, and our son, Simon Raoul Leslie, has brought unparalleled joy by providing a new dimension to my life.

PART ONE

JUST A SURVIVOR

Chapter One

EARLY RECOLLECTIONS OF MY FAMILY

My Maternal Keve Family

It may be politically incorrect to start by talking about race, but ethnically I was born Jewish. Both sides of the family were Jewish, and I remain so, although not observant. My family had not converted even under emergency conditions, even when they were repeatedly threatened with violence and were in immediate danger of extinction. One of my mother's emphatically stated comments was: 'I shall kill, cheat and lie if necessary, but I shall not abandon my faith'.

If this sounds like an affirmation of religious zeal, it was not. My family were not at all religious. In 1919, when my grandfather was offered an affidavit to go the United States, his wife declared that she was not going, she was a *Hungarian* and her life was to be in that land. Misguided comments like this were not uncommon in her generation; it was – in hindsight – a narrow, incorrect and ultimately fatal attitude. Had my family, or half of it, emigrated at that time, biologically it would have been impossible for me to exist, although my mother's genes would have been propagated by some other offspring. He may have been a better writer.

My maternal grandfather, Ferenc Keve, was a urological surgeon. In the early part of the century and after World War One, urology was closely involved with venereal disease. His major interests were disease manifestations and treatment, and he was also interested in common skin disorders. Some of his papers from the *Budapest Medical Journal* are in my collection, as he contributed to the medical literature of the times. He served throughout the First World War as a surgeon-colonel in the armies of the Austro-Hungarian monarchy, and travelled, accompanied by this family, in occupied territories such as Poland and Russia. Although a Jew, emancipation enabled him to complete his university course with distinction.

His family hailed from a small town called Túroczszentmárton in Slovakia, which was then part of Hungary. Over 120 years after his birth, a prisoner of war captured in World War Two, who came from the same village many decades later, was repatriated from the Soviet Union; that is the only time I had ever heard the name of that town. After World War One Grandfather's further advancement was limited by his origins, as Jews were highly discriminated against by this time. Hungary was the first country in Europe to limit their enrolment in universities and regulate their numbers in professions. Grandfather became head of a major health insurance provider, a prestigious appointment, but without academic involvement. He suffered from diabetes and, regrettably, cut his finger during an operation and died of sepsis three years before I was born. He was revered by his family. I was named after him, and whenever I performed well, even at primary school, I was reminded of grandfather's achievements. I know little else of the Keve family background except that they came from humble beginnings.

Two Family Houses

In 1944, Grandfather's only brother, Miklós, was foolish enough to walk down the street in the early days of the Nazi occupation, and was never seen again. The house where Miklós and his family lived in Ujpest (the extensive, flat part of Budapest east of the Danube River) was a large apartment building, with a stationery store off the street. I never went inside the building – I did not even know its address – but I knew my mother and grandfather had a share in the property. In fact Grandfather bought it after World War One in order to provide security for his family and his brother. The house consisted of twenty-four apartments; we received some rental from it. In 1944 it was confiscated by the Nazi puppet government of Hungary. The entry on the title simply said: 'Owner Jewish – property seized by the law of date XX, of paragraph YY.' After Liberation, it was restored for a brief period, but after fleeing Hungary in 1949, we lost all rights and, as stateless persons, were dispossessed.

We lived in the old city called Óbuda (the smaller, hilly part of the city west of the river), and I distinctly remember later moving to another flat in a garden suburb, where we had an upstairs apartment. Grandmother lived below in her own rented flat. The concierge, who had a son of my age, later played an ignoble role in our future. When I was two years old, the ceiling of our living room in Óbuda caved in. Fortunately my cot was moved to another room some hours before. An early portent of things to come perhaps, as ten years later at the moment of Liberation, something similar happened.

My Maternal Grandmother

Anna Keve, my maternal grandmother, played a dominant role in my upbringing. She was very close to me and looked after me when Mother had to go to work, assuming the role of the breadwinner, after increasingly severe racial laws led to my father's dismissal. Anna was trying to contribute to the household by knitting exquisite pullovers by hand, which supplemented her pension. When I once referred to her as a 'knitting lady', she became quite indignant and exclaimed that she was a surgeon's widow. I learnt my lesson. She was enlightened, egalitarian and once, when a school friend referred to another poor child as a proletarian, grandmother forbade me to invite the snob home again.

Grandmother spoke four languages and read me stories whilst knitting. She also taught me most of what I know about the family. Her father owned a huge paper wholesale business in Budapest. The family house was so spacious that in the courtyard, in the heart of Budapest, carts drawn by six horses were able to turn around with deliveries of stationery. The family got into financial difficulties during the Depression and Anna's two brothers, who were honourable men, refused to declare bankruptcy. They accepted their liabilities, paid up to the last cent, but became poverty stricken as a result. Grandmother was a 'living encyclopaedia' of names and dates about the family; all that knowledge has vanished forever. I merely recall fragments. Anna died of leukaemia on 21 April 1944, four weeks after the Nazi occupation. The date and the funeral almost ended in fatal consequences, as I shall relate later.

Great-uncle Nándor died when I was four; his widow, who had been an actress, was tempestuous and theatrical. They had one son, whom they adored, who later became a victim when forcibly taken to the eastern front in Ukraine. Great-uncle Jani was also one of my favourites. A natural mathematician, he taught me the concept of right and left, but he declined mentally in his later years and ended up in an old people's home. He used to visit us for dinner once a week, and I recall him as a gentle but sad old man. His son Feri became one of my closest relatives, and one of the last surviving ones. Although the Keve family was extensive, with branches in Czechoslovakia, Yugoslavia, and in provincial Hungary, the intervention of German jackboots wiped out my systematic knowledge of the family's members, as sixty lost their lives. As a result my memory is confined to those whom I could recall from the first eight years of my life.

My Paternal Family

My grandfather on my father's side, Zsigmond Vajda, was a very humble man, who was able to educate two sons to university and professional levels on a modest salary as a bookkeeper. Born in Karcag in provincial Hungary, I recall him holding me on his knee every weekend and reading me stories and poetry. This is the main memory I possess of him. He was a non-assertive man, whose passing in May 1944 led to another tragedy.

Grandmother Rózsi was a beautiful woman, who even in her final years retained her classic dark elegance and strong facial appearance. She was the lady of the house, adored by my father and his brother, and she kept a traditional household. She was a Mendelsohn, allegedly related to the composer, Felix Mendelsohn-Bartholdy; I certainly think fondly of a possible relationship with the composer, and even more so of the music he created. My introduction to classical music – my first vinyl record – was the Mendelsohn Violin Concerto. It remains my favourite piece of violin music, and it was played, quite unexpectedly, at the funeral of a dear friend, the last man to see my father alive. At that funeral the song of the Hebrew Slaves by Verdi was played as well, again perhaps as a mark of respect for the slave labourers incarcerated in the camps, and perhaps as a mark of respect to my father, a fellow prisoner and friend of the deceased, a long time ago.

Our Family's Relationship to Judaism

We lacked any close affinity to religion and were classed as neologs, or liberal Jews. Other members of the family, on the paternal side, maintained a closer tie with Jewish tradition and Judaism. My grandfather asked that when he died there be no words in Hebrew on his tombstone, although he was named Efráim at birth. On the other hand my paternal uncle, an adoring relative, who was adored in return, was very observant, putting on the t'fillim each day. My grandmother ran a kosher kitchen.

As in most things a compromise was necessary, and although I gained my first contact with groups of children in a German speaking kindergarten (run incidentally by German Jewish ladies, who were refugees from Nazism), it was followed soon after by starting in a Jewish primary school, which I attended for eighteen months. There I began to read Hebrew and learnt about traditional Jewish history and culture, lessons tragically undercut by the German 'invasion' of Hungary. Occupation is a better term, as there was no military action and rather an outpouring of affection, rather than resistance, from the populace. Immediately afterwards the persecution of the civilian Jewish population began and with it our personal Holocaust.

Chapter Two

THE PLIGHT OF HUNGARIAN JEWRY

Historical Anti-Semitism in Hungary

In recalling the various aspects of the Holocaust, it is difficult to express the overwhelming extent of the damage and destruction that a racist ideology has wreaked upon the world, and foremost upon the Jewish people, of whom six million were brutally murdered in the years 1933–1945. Trying to understand both those who eliminated the Jews and those who tried to save them can only be attempted in the overall context of the statistics, timetables and logistics of mass murder. Here I shall briefly sketch the situation as it prevailed at that time in Hungary.

For centuries there had been conflict between Jews and non-Jews in Central Europe, although the intensity of anti-Semitism was less than elsewhere. It appears to me the further east one travelled, the standard of living, education, tolerance, and climate for co-existence worsened. In Hungary the conflict exploded after the First World War. After the defeat of the Austro-Hungarian monarchy, the country was ruled briefly by a Communist dictatorship, which contained a disproportionate representation of Jewish revolutionaries. Nationalistic counter-revolutionary forces, led by a former monarchist admiral, Miklós Horthy, overthrew this regime. This person nominated himself head of state.

Horthy's first acts consisted of countenancing the murder of Jews, socialists and other political opponents, ostensibly by extremists, but with his direct permission. Sixty years after the Second World War Horthy is posthumously (at least they cannot resurrect him) subject to a process of being made respectable again, a disgrace beyond parallel. It was this weak, despicable accomplice in genocide who introduced the first racial laws in Europe in 1920. These laws excluded Jews from universities and paved the way for the so-called Jewish laws, successively enacted by willing support from Parliament in 1938, 1940, and 1941. These acts eased the way to Hitler's final solution, with considerable, enthusiastic Hungarian participation.

The climate of anti-Semitism in Hungary was markedly aggravated after the rise of the Nazis to power in Germany in 1933. Already in the 1920s and early 1930s Hungary was ruled by a government of nationalist right-wing views, which was under the influence of the Regent, Admiral Horthy, who already had an unsavoury record. The lives of Jews were made difficult by a general climate of vilification by the right-wing press, which agitated and threatened them. My father was beaten up by Nazi vigilantes at the university and had to abandon his course. After the establishment of a more extremely anti-Semitic succession of Prime Ministers from 1933 onwards, the country found itself drawn into Hitler's orbit. Support by the Nazis of the *Volksdeutschen* (people of German descent living in Hungary) and financing local Fascists resulted in increasing pressure on Jews, which was formalised by the later Racial Laws. These were of increasing severity; the last law went even further than the Nüremberg Laws in its racial definition of who was a Jew.

The Horthy Regime in 1941–1944

The Jewish population of Hungary was of the order of 400,000 when in 1938 and 1940 Germany and Italy, as part of Hitler's so-called Vienna Awards, allotted to Hungary parts of Czechoslovakia, Northern Transylvania taken from Romania, parts of Yugoslavia and areas of Transcarpathia. This territorial gain totally bound Hungary to Hitler. It also had the unexpected effect of doubling the number of Jewish inhabitants in Hungary: the largest concentrations of Jews were living in the areas now annexed by Hungary. These people were never regarded by anti-Semites as Hungarian citizens, but as foreign Jews, fit only for slaughter. In 1941 Hungary joined the German invasion of Yugoslavia. Subsequently, in January 1942, the Hungarian army, gendarmerie and police committed an atrocity in Novi Sad, killing around four thousand people, including some twelve hundred Jews. According to the historian Zvonimir Golubović, the victims were driven out onto the frozen Danube River, which was then shelled, causing them to drown. This action was so bestial that the Hungarian Government decided to prosecute the perpetrators, but later allowed them to flee to Germany.

As the war in the east progressed, a manhunt was conducted in Hungary with the aim of deporting Jews whose papers could not prove that they had lived in Hungary continuously since the First World War. This action was aimed at many Slovakian and Polish Jews, who had fled to Hungary to escape the Final Solution in their own countries. Hungary was indeed a place of refuge at this time, as the physical existence of Jews was not yet immediately under threat. The Hungarian anti-Jewish laws did not prescribe the Jewish star, but were largely concerned with expropriating Jewish property, and restricting the capacity of Jews to earn a living. As a result many Jews became destitute. Subsequently, twenty thousand so-called 'foreign' Jews were deported to Kamenets-Podolski (a town today in the Ukraine) by Hungarian authorities, against the wishes of Eichmann, who did not wish to concern himself with small numbers. These Jews were massacred by SS troops under General Jeckeln and by Hungarian engineering battalions.

Beginning in 1939 a law made it compulsory for Jewish males aged from seventeen to sixty, almost without regard to their fitness or health, to be called up for compulsory, para-military, slave labour service. They had to wear their own clothes, and were unarmed and harshly treated. About 60,000 men, the cream of Hungarian Jewry, were in this category; the majority were taken to the eastern front in the Ukraine, where they were grossly maltreated and humiliated, and made to carry out inhuman tasks, such as being taken to minefields to blow up the mines ahead of the Hungarian Army. Most of these tragic 'labour servicemen' were murdered. They were treated more brutally by their Hungarian guards and by the SS than the Jews of other countries. These slave labourers were starved and brutalised, made to do menial tasks without equipment, and then tortured for the amusement of the guards, who made no secret of their desire not to see any Jew in their custody survive.

Other Jews, some enjoying protection by neutral countries, were spared from the eastern front, but attacked within Hungary by the Germans and Hungarian Arrow Cross militia in the last six months of the war. In addition many slave labourers captured by the Russians had to endure despicable treatment at the hands of the Soviets in gulags and POW camps. The Russians often gave preferential treatment to Nazis; Jews had to fend off Nazi POWs as well as their Soviet captors. In contrast there are many stories of liberation and wonderful treatment by the Red Army, especially if the captives were able to speak Slav languages, or were fortunate enough to meet Russian Jewish Army officers.

Several thousand Hungarian Jewish slave labourers were sent to the copper mines of Bor in Yugoslavia. Delivered to the Todt organisation, a Third Reich civil and military engineering group, they were worked to exhaustion. Survivors were eventually sent back to Hungary in two columns of two thousand men each. The first column was attacked by ethnic German militia in Yugoslavia and was eventually almost completely wiped out. The second column survived the march back to Hungary in 1944, but were rounded up by the ultra-right-wing Arrow Cross units and deported to concentration camps where the majority were murdered. Many others were deported by the Hungarians towards the west, as a result of Auschwitz death marches. This group included my father, murdered at Ebensee.

The Situation of Hungarian Jews before 1944

Hungary was an ally of Hitler, and sent troops to the war against the Soviet Union; it was not actively occupied by the Nazis until late in the war. Until 1944 the Jews of Hungary, although subjected to privations and hardships, were not in danger of death and were not confined to ghettoes, nor were they compelled to wear the Jewish star which in the long term became the mark of death, as it enabled the Nazis to identify them, restrict their movements and eventually deport them to the death camps. After its introduction, removal of the Star of David was punishable by deportation or death.

The increasingly severe Jewish Laws ensured that many families became destitute as they could not secure employment. Our family struggled on. The relatively long period of freedom enjoyed by the Hungarian Jews became a source of envy, and later contempt, for many other European Jews. The contempt was deserved because the Jews of Hungary in their unbelievable stupidity believed that what happened in Poland, in the Baltic states and in Russia could never happen to them as 'Hungarians'. They felt certain of the protection of the Regent, Admiral Horthy, but he was a feeble, ageing, spineless toady of Hitler, whose effective rule was virtually abrogated after being confronted by the Germans. He eventually handed over his Jewish population, seemingly quite willingly, except for a last remnant in Budapest. The final reprieve for the remains of Hungarian Jewry was not due to any Axis generosity, but to requests and warnings from the Allies, the Pope and the Swedish King.

It is certainly not true that the Hungarian Jews lived in luxury while the other Jews of Europe were gassed. Males were taken to slave labour, where they were treated abominably, as we have seen. A statement attributed to the commander of one of these slave labour service battalions reads as follows: 'I shall see to it that the Jews return only as names in my briefcase'. Of 60,000 Hungarian Jewish slave labourers, some 45,000 perished, including many members of my family and friends.

The German Takeover

Nineteen-forty-four was the last full year of the war. On 19 March 1944 the Germans occupied Hungary. No shots were fired. The Eichmann *Einsatzkommando*, charged with organising and facilitating the murder of Jews, followed on the heels of the Wehrmacht. They were better prepared to accomplish their tasks than any group in Hungary or Germany pursuing genuine war aims. Within twenty-four hours thousands of Jews were arrested, their selection based on information carefully listed and documented. They were taken to internment camps, and soon deported to Auschwitz. The repressive measures taken to implement the timetable for genocide went into effect rapidly – freezing of assets, restrictions on travel, expulsion from jobs, handing over of valuables, and prohibition of mixing with Aryans.

On 5 April 1944 wearing the Star of David became compulsory. This was a major blow. It had to be affixed so tightly that a pencil inserted behind the star could not dislodge it. Wearing the star invited humiliation and terror, marking in rapid sequence the process of destruction. I recall our family debating whether to buy Jewish stars at exorbitant prices from stores owned by Nazi sympathizers, for example, Nagykovacsi's, who profiteered from our misery, or to make the stars ourselves. We opted for the latter.

The Germans, under Eichmann, the Hungarian butchers Endre and Baky, and the gendarmerie, were vigorously supported by the Hungarian administrative machinery, from army personnel to judges, from Parliament to civil servants, as well as many unknown informers, denouncers, and agitators. Such people raided Jewish functions, attacked Jewish funerals, conducted raids on public transport, taking their captives to Auschwitz. Prominent figures were arrested from the day of occupation onwards: some sent postcards from Auschwitz to calm their relatives.

The Deportation of Provincial Jews

From March 1944 the Jews of Hungary started their march to hell. In six weeks the Germans completed the Final Solution for Jews in all the provinces of Hungary; only Budapest remained. Provincial ghettos were set up. Deportations started from the eastern part of the country on May 15, rapidly followed by the rest thereafter. As we learnt later, Jews travelling on trains were arrested and thrown into ghettoes in their vicinity, which was my father's tragic fate.

After the establishment of ghettos in all cities and provincial towns, Jews were concentrated under inhuman conditions. In fact the phrase 'inhuman conditions' does not adequately convey the full horror of their situation – the despair, brutality, torture, cold, hunger, lack of sanitation and medical facilities, forced abandonment of homes, breakup of families, beatings, rapes, electric shock treatment and gross overcrowding, combined with the fear and haunting suspicion of death hanging over them and their loved ones.

Between 15 May and 30 June 1944, according to official German figures, 437,000 Jews were transported for 'resettlement', the German doublespeak for being taken to a train, eighty people to a cattle truck, so tightly cramped that people could barely breathe or sit. Transported in the heat for up to three days without water or food, taken off the train by armed guards and dogs, herded to a ramp, and then walked to a room, undressed and, after the door was closed, allowed to wait in order to warm up, and then suffocated by cyanide poured down a hatch, carefully and scientifically designed by the Germans, with typical German precision, to the last detail. So ended the lives of my relatives.

The remaining Jews of Hungary, still alive but trembling with fear, were predominantly in Budapest. We knew what to expect. I knew at the age of eight and a half. Hence our desperate attempts to fend off this fate, aided by fortune, by non-Jewish friends, by taking risks, by Raoul Wallenberg, and ultimately by the Red Army of Liberation.

The Deportation of Budapest Jews

Prior to deportation from the capital, internment camps were set up near Budapest, for example at Kistarcsa, from where deportations continued until July. As the next measure the outer suburbs of Budapest were deported, including Ujpest and Pestszenterzsebet, from which my relatives were taken. The Gestapo arrested many opposition politicians and unionists, but there was no organised resistance. In Budapest, many children were hidden in monasteries and convents, and many Jewish people were helped by friends who were horrified by events. These people risked their lives, as the Gestapo was active and there were many denunciations, more than elsewhere in Europe.

Listening to enemy radio broadcasts were forbidden; Jewish people had to surrender their radios, and their assets were frozen. Curfews were imposed. The scheduled date of the deportations from the capital was 2 August 1944, later postponed to 29 August. The Regent Horthy was warned about the consequences if he permitted further deportations after the tragedy of the provincial Jews. The Allies subjected Budapest to massive bombing raids, which led to the postponement and eventual cessation of the planned deportations. However, Horthy's feeble attempt to seek an armistice led to a coup d'état. On 15 October the extreme right wing local Arrow Cross militia seized power and embarked on a reign of terror. The Arrow Cross shot thousands of victims and forced over forty thousand Jews to go on death marches, during which many perished. Some say as many as 20,000 people, mainly Jews, were murdered by the Arrow Cross, who often dumped the bodies of their victims into the Danube.

Raoul Wallenberg arrived in July, about three months before the Arrow Cross putsch, too late to help the provincial deportees, but able to set in place an organisation to exert maximum efforts to save the Jews of Budapest. Wallenberg and other emissaries from neutral countries succeeded in saving many lives. Their names have become legendary. Their deeds, and the miraculous escapes many people had, will be dwelt on in more detail later.

The Siege of Budapest

Budapest was besieged by massive Red Army formations as the Soviet Union made its push westward to eliminate the retreating German armies. The siege of Budapest, which lasted from December 1944 to February 1945, contributed to the local death toll. During this time, the Jewish population of Budapest was effectively halved. Of the initial 200,000 Jews estimated to live there, about 50,000 were deported, together with some labour service battalions taken in death marches to Auschwitz or to be worked to death building fortifications in Austria. In addition, many people died in the siege itself as a result of bombing and artillery fire, and as a result of starvation, disease and neglect.

Of the 119,000 Jewish survivors in Budapest, about 69,000 were living in the general ghetto of Budapest, which was saved primarily by the efforts of Wallenberg, even though most survivors never met him. Wallenberg blackmailed the German general in Budapest into countermanding an order to raze the ghetto. This is the true story of the rescue of the ghetto, told to me personally by Ambassador Per Anger, a colleague of Wallenberg, a man I believe in above all others. Sixty thousand people survived as a result of these actions.

There were possibly thirty thousand Jews who survived as a direct result of the *Schutzpasses* (forged protection papers) issued by the neutral states, Sweden, Switzerland, Portugal, Spain, the Vatican, El Salvador, and by the Swedish and International Red Cross. Many Jews used false papers, such as baptismal certificates and university admission papers. The tireless representatives of these humane nations intervened on behalf of the Jews, establishing a so-called 'international protected ghetto', based on bluff and fiction. There was some resistance: certainly armed Jewish Zionist resistance groups attacked Nazis and liberated some intended victims. Many Jews owe their lives to Righteous Gentiles, who hid them in cellars, flats, caves, monasteries and other buildings or on farms. This was similar to the rescue attempts experienced by Jews in the rest of occupied Europe.

Chapter Three

EIGHT CLOSE SHAVES

Deportations

To imagine that a former lice-infested vagabond, an amateur painter of watercolours, a man with a pallid face and hysterical oratory, could take over a so-called civilised country, and form a political grouping of like-minded discontents is bad enough. But to predict that he would gain an ever-increasing audience, focusing on racism, hate and revanchism, and eventually on world domination and mass murder, is an incredible scenario. On top of this, to actually accomplish some of these aims, including launching the world into war and in the process having six million Jews, his projected scapegoat and imaginary enemy, murdered, along with tens of millions of other people murdered or otherwise killed, is a totally horrific prospect. But this is precisely what happened, as we all know.

Hitler nearly got me. Not once but eight times. This is the story of these escapes, listed in the order they happened.

After the German occupation of Hungary in March 1944, a puppet, right-wing government was installed whose major task was a speedy implementation of Hitler's Final Solution. It was to be carried out by the Hungarian government and its state apparatus, supervised by the Eichmann *Sonderkommando* of a mere two hundred SS men. For this purpose Hungary was divided into six zones, and, as in Poland and other occupied countries, the process followed a well-established pattern. Jews were collected in country centres, their property was looted, they were then forced into ghettoes in the larger cities, and after a few weeks of starvation, humiliation and further looting, they were crowded into cattle trucks and deported to Auschwitz. In seven weeks provincial Jews were deported in an unspeakably cruel manner to the gas chambers and crematoria. Five out of the six districts were dispatched, two thousand humans per train, five trains per day, 300,000 in a month. Provincial Hungary became *Judenrein* (cleansed of Jews) in six weeks.

Only the Jews of the capital remained, where 200,000 of them, about a third of the total, lived. The deportation of Budapest Jews was left to the last, perhaps as it was the most difficult problem to deal with, due to sheer numbers and difficulties of transport. The city had an overall population of about one million people, for the most part living in apartments. The diameter of the city area was about ten kilometres. The outer suburbs on the rim of the circle were about six kilometres from the centre of the city. The standard of houses and the affluence of the people inhabiting these outer suburbs varied significantly. Of the Jews, some were working class, others wealthy middle class.

The trains started rolling on 15 July, and took 50,000 Jews from the outer suburbs of Budapest to their death in Auschwitz. Deportation from these suburbs claimed the lives of my uncle from Ujpest, and two cousins and their mother from Szenterzsébet. The father of this family had already been arrested as a prominent Jew, and deported some weeks earlier. The rest of the city's Jewish population was scheduled for embarkation over the following two weeks, but a little later the deportations were postponed, by order of the nominal ruler of the country, Horthy, as a result of appeals from a group of neutral countries, and from the Western Allies, who threatened severe retribution if they continued. The postponement was also possibly influenced by the receipt in the West of the Auschwitz Protocols, a description of the killing machinery written by two escapees from that extermination camp. Other factors were a fear by Horthy of a planned putsch, thought to be planned by Nazi sympathizers in the gendarmerie, who wished to remove him from office.

Thus in terms of time, we were only one week away from being conveyed to Auschwitz, where no child under thirteen, as I was, had the remotest chance of escaping immediate gassing. In terms of distance, we had been living three kilometres from suburbs which had already been cleared of Jews, and subsequently we lived about two kilometres from Ujpest, which was by then also cleared of Jews by the combined savagery of the Hungarian and German authorities. We were therefore one week and two kilometres from deportation, an exceedingly close brush with death, if you consider the length of World War Two. We escaped by a frighteningly narrow margin, but it resulted in survival instead of burning in the crematoria.

That was our first escape.

The Funeral

Although Budapest was the last locality on the list to target for deportations, the police started arresting Jews at railway stations and at funerals. Funerals were usually attended by families, and hence were a good hunting ground for the police. The Jewish cemetery of Rákoskeresztúr was thirty-five minutes away by tram from the centre of the city, one tram stop past the Aryan cemetery. Because Jewish funerals were well attended even during these times, the police lay in wait, searching for intended victims at the cemetery gates. After a single example of such arrests, news spread like wildfire that those attending a funeral were putting their lives at immediate risk. But this did not deter most of the mourners.

My maternal grandmother died on 21 April 1944. I recall my mother being warned by relatives of the great danger she would run by attending the funeral. And I remember to this day, seventy years later, my mother looking with defiant pride and total determination straight at relatives who were warning her, and saying: 'You do not seriously imagine me failing to attend my mother's funeral, do you?' But they all agreed that the child must not go. I refused to accept that and went with my mother to the funeral, the first of many dangers we were to share in the future.

At the funeral we saw police who were waiting to arrest mourners. But at the precise moment when the funeral service was to about to begin, an air raid alarm sounded. The gravediggers fled, the gendarmes fled, the police hid in shelters. My family picked up the coffin and in total silence and with great dignity took the coffin to the grave and buried grandmother. I do not remember a single word spoken. We returned to the entrance of the cemetery, boarded a tram, and returned, unmolested, to our homes in the city.

Fifty years later, Erwin Révai, a close friend and systems engineer now living in Sweden, told me that under exactly the same circumstances (except that there was no air raid) his poor mother was taken and deported to her death after a funeral. His father tried for the next ten years to seek information from anyone who could shed some light on her fate.

The Gestapo

By June 1944, Jews in Budapest were already confined to specified areas, mostly in so-called 'Jewish houses' marked with the Star of David. They had only restricted access to areas of what the Nazis regarded as the 'Aryan' city population. There were curfews, a yellow star had to be worn by everyone including children above the age of four, and the necessities of life were hard to obtain. Radios had long been confiscated, as Jews were not to be informed of external events. The house where we lived was a Jewish hospital outside the ghetto. We had a radio, which was used regularly to monitor the BBC, but we had no transmitters. My mother was the principal person listening to the broadcasts, because she spoke English better than anyone else.

The SD, the *Sicherheitsdienst* or Security Service, a lethal arm of the Gestapo, had mobile vans monitoring the area to try to catch people in the act of listening. Our radio was located in the loft. Suddenly the Gestapo arrived, led by an officer in black uniform with armed men, accusing the staff of the hospital of sending illegal transmissions to the enemy. My mother hastily hid the receiver, and then confronted the Gestapo. In perfectly literate High German, which she had spoken since childhood, she challenged the dreaded SD to search the place but denied vehemently any wrongdoing and succeeded in getting her story across. A search was made, nothing found, and the Nazis left.

I recall this was a summer's day; every person had to assemble in the front courtyard in the sun, witness the discussion and wait for the result of the search. What would have happened if she had not been believed, or if the radio had been discovered, need no elaboration – it would have meant immediate execution for all assembled.

The Military Barracks

On 15 October 1944, the Regent of Hungary, Horthy, asked the Allies for an armistice. He made a broadcast, stating the war was lost, and Hitler had let down his collaborators. Horthy wished to end the bloodshed. The Jews responded with jubilation by tearing off the hated yellow star. But Horthy acted prematurely; he had not backed his proclamation with military force. Hitler sent in his SS commando led by the notorious Otto Skorzeny, the regent's son was arrested, and Horthy surrendered his power to the Hungarian Nazis. Jews like us were reported to the new extremist Arrow Cross regime for the crime of having removed the Star of David, a crime punishable by death according to their laws.

The next day, 16 October 1944, was a date I well remember; two days after my ninth birthday, and a date that should be on my gravestone. A patrol of Arrow Cross servicemen arrived at the hospital to investigate and a shouting match ensued. My mother was very brave and defended our removal of the Star, referring to the speech by the highest authority, Horthy. I had to hysterically beg her to shut up, as they were on the point of shooting her. The Horthy proclamation, even the mention of his name, added fuel to the fire. Horthy was discredited, and his name brought violent curses to the lips of our attackers, who threatened to shoot us on the spot. Finally they asked us to produce our clothes with the yellow stars. As we had two minutes to report back to them, we rushed off and found the jackets with stars torn off. We hastily tried to put them back on with safety pins. They laughed when they saw the pitiful attempts we had made, and shouted orders to march us off to their headquarters. We all understood what this meant. The Arrow Cross men said: 'We are not taking the child.' But the child insisted and joined the march. (After this episode, no moral victory over the subsequent seventy years could be equal to that single decision, since fear of that magnitude does not exist any longer.)

Arriving at the neighbouring Albrecht Military Barracks, and escorted by the Arrow Cross, we were marched through the front gate, and taken to a wall, with a machine gun facing it about five metres away. We were lined up. One of the women fainted. I did not know the reason. I was told that the Nyilas (Arrow Cross militia) were debating whether to finish us off on the spot or to take us to the Danube. I recall weighing up the alternatives – maybe they would change their minds and take us to the ghetto? Suddenly the situation changed dramatically. Civilians arrived and the Arrow Cross group were huddled in a debate. Following this we were quietly escorted back to the hospital. This was I believe the result of Wallenberg in action. Seventy years later I have tears in my eye as I recollect this story.

From another source comes a story of a strange coincidence of time and place. Erwin Forrester has been head of the Wallenberg Committee in Sydney since 1983. In 1944 he was a slave labourer stationed at Fertőrákos, a name associated with atrocities against labour servicemen. Though guarded by a Hitler *Jugend* (youth) detachment at this late stage of the war, he escaped from his unit on the way to Auschwitz, because a soldier told him to run as they would all be killed. He was caught and taken to the Albrecht Barracks in Budapest on the corner of Szabolcs and Aréna Streets, the same military arsenal used as the Arrow Cross headquarters from October 1944. Erwin was put in a cell awaiting court-martial with three others who had escaped from slave labour.

At the hearing, the first person was asked by the military judge if he was a Jew. Yes, he said. Escaped? Yes, he said. Verdict: Shoot him! They took him outside and shot him. Second person, similarly. Third person: No, I am a Swede! How come? I have a passport to prove it. Show us! He produced a *Schutzpass*, a protection paper. The tribunal conferred and said: We'll decide on this later. Take him back to the cell. Then came Forrester. Jewish? No, I am a Swede. Show us your papers! Erwin replied his papers were in the hands of Mr Wallenberg at the Swedish Embassy – please ring him. They did so, spoke to Wallenberg, asking him if he knew this man and whether he had papers for him. Yes, said Wallenberg, asking for his date of birth, eye colour, address and height. They told Wallenberg, who wrote down the details as they spoke. Soon after a man unknown to Forrester appeared at the Albrecht Barracks and said to him: We shall save you. It was Raoul Wallenberg, who did save my friend, as Forrester was released and, in time, escaped.

In later conversations I mentioned to Erwin the physical appearance of the barracks building, in front of which we were lined up facing the machine gun. A two-storey, stark, white-walled barracks, on the left of the parade ground, with a tank near the main gate, the gate being ochre yellow, abutting on Szabolcs Street. Erwin replied quietly: 'It was inside this same building that I was held in the condemned cell, when Wallenberg came in and said '*Wir werden Sie noch retten!*' ('We shall save you!') The same building, the same saviour.

Where to Hide?

The same day, shivering with fear as the realisation of the proximity of death stalking us was brought home, we saw an ambulance pull up at the front gate. It was customary for an ambulance to have a driver, a doctor and a policeman as part of the crew. On this occasion they brought in one of the many suicide cases. We noted the policeman, and in our jittery state we feared that the Arrow Cross had made a mistake in releasing us, and that they had arrived to re-claim their victims. We had Aryan (Roman Catholic) papers, and Mother and I jumped out of a ground floor window and started walking, carrying a bag containing our belongings, ready for such an emergency. We did not wear the yellow star, as we intended to blend in with the city's population, or in other words 'go underground'. The first grave risk was that just outside the hospital, along the road bordering the Albrecht Barracks, military guards were on duty every twenty yards. They may well have seen us returning from the march a few hours earlier with the other people who had been plucked from danger. We could have been recognised, but we took the chance.

We had some money, so we ate in cafes, but on the first night took a grave risk by moving into an apartment belonging to a relative, which had been sealed as 'Jewish property'. It was a lawyer's office and we had to wait until after dark to enter through the internal staircase and gangway, so as not to be seen by any neighbours. We slept in an armchair near the window and watched the Jewish population being marched into a new ghetto, maltreated, abused and having rubbish thrown at them. Next day we just loitered around – restaurants, Danube boat journeys, cinemas and fear. A lot of fear.

That night we had a new idea. A former domestic of ours lived in a rented room in the city. We called in on her. She was magnificently generous; she let us in, did not betray us, let us have her bed, her only one. The two-room flat was tenanted by other people, and she was a sub-tenant. Mother explained that we were refugees from the Allied bombing in the provinces. The lady of the house accepted this, but at two o'clock that night her husband came home. He did not like our story and decided to check it out. So in the early hours of the morning Mother had to undergo a session of being questioned by him about our history, my father's military rank (he was in Auschwitz), his position, unit, last news and exact details of the bombing we had suffered.

I pretended to be asleep. I knew that I could not provide a story consistent with the story Mother had delivered. When the interview was over I whispered to my mother: 'I did not know you could tell so many lies'. Next day the landlady's son was playing with some toys representing a Nativity scene and in my innocence, I nearly brought disaster upon us. I asked: 'What is this you are playing with?' After this Mother thought we had better depart, and we did so promptly. It was just in time, as we found out later that the landlord who used to come home late at night was an Arrow Cross trooper, and spent his evenings shooting Jews on the banks of the Danube.

Interposed at this point is a story I discovered in the archives of the Budapest Jewish community only sixty-five years after the events described. It appears from a deposition made by the Director of the hospital which sheltered us, that the same afternoon that we were rescued by Wallenberg and returned to the protected house on his word under neutral protection, the Arrow Cross were not quite as fully deceived as it had appeared. They returned to check out the documents of people who were rescued, but fortunately they were pacified and did not look for them again. But our fear was of exactly that scenario. Hence our hasty departure was fully justified.

A Raid in Winter

On 3 January 1945 there was a great commotion at the hospital after we had returned following our feeble attempt to survive using false papers. It was another Arrow Cross raid. Arrow Cross servicemen in civilian clothes, wearing the armbands of that organisation, with rifles levelled at women and children and cursing violently, herded several hundred terrified Jews into the basement. In the freezing cold winter night, they made us put our hands up, swearing and abusing us constantly. (It is difficult to keep one's hands in the air, as they get tired.) After what seemed an eternity, new orders were issued: 'Get your papers; we must check all the documents.'

My cousin and his wife shared a small room with us and about eight other people, but we were separated from them in the line-up, as there were three hundred people living in that small, twenty-bed obstetrics hospital. When the order was given for everybody to collect their documents, my mother and I decided not to comply. Mother whispered to me – and I remember this over the passage of seventy years: 'We shall not present ourselves for documentation. We shall hide.' My answer was simply: 'Where?' She replied: 'In the bathroom, behind the information desk.' For once I did not argue, nor 'know' better. Although I had often thought of such a contingency, like hiding in case of a raid, I had always thought that the broom cupboard next to the bathroom was preferable to hide in, but the differences were marginal, and obviously this was not the time for a debate.

We rushed upstairs directly into the bathroom and hid ourselves in a clothes locker made up of multiple cupboards, with a series of small punctured apertures on the doors for air. We stayed there in the terrible cold, hearing no noise from the main part of the building. When we emerged, we met wailing, distraught friends and relatives, whose families had been taken, never to return. We had been very close to extinction again. As we found out later, the victims were taken to the Arrow Cross headquarters, humiliated, robbed and then murdered. One battered survivor returned and confirmed the story.

The Alice Weiss Hospital where we lived was a so-called 'protected house'. It claimed extra-territoriality under the flags and emblems of the neutral legations, and the International and Swedish Red Cross. Most people had no individual protection papers, but were housed there as part of a collective attempt to offer such people protection. A meeting of a cousin of mine with Raoul Wallenberg came about as a result of his frantic pleas to save his mother, and being told that there was only one man who could do anything at all in this living hell for these poor abandoned people, and that was Raoul Wallenberg.

So the next morning, 3 January 1945, in Nazi occupied Budapest, nine days before our Liberation by the Red Army, my cousin, who was about thirty years old, made a phone call. He spoke to someone in an office and requested an appointment on urgent business. Told to come at once, he took his overcoat, removed his Jewish star and walked to another part of the city at that time under siege.

On arrival he met a man who was of medium build, about his own age, who spoke German with a strange accent, was very friendly, approachable and easy to communicate with. He listened to my cousin's story that five hours earlier the Arrow Cross had broken into the protected hospital where we lived, lined up everybody in the basement, selected thirty-five people and dragged them away. My cousin reported that the Director of the hospital wanted to know if anything could be done to retrieve them. The young man, who was very tired, and looked exhausted and sad, listened. He replied he regretted that it was a hopeless task. The people taken were no longer alive, as the Arrow Cross murdered Jews indiscriminately. After dragging them away and robbing them, they would have been shot and pushed into the river Danube.

My cousin broke down and cried, telling the man that his own mother and a number of other relatives were in the group. The young man stood up, came over to him, put his arm on his shoulder and said: 'I know and feel your personal tragedy, and I am terribly sorry to be unable to help, I wish I could help you. The murderers are already after me as well, hunting for me and I have great difficulty evading them. I really feel very sorry.' That man, aged thirty-two at the time, was Raoul Wallenberg. He disappeared exactly fourteen days after this episode. My cousin tells the story that he could feel the compassion and distress this man felt for people he had never met. It is an enduring testament of the kindness and decency that Raoul Wallenberg left with my cousin, as indeed he left with the thousands of people who came in contact with him, who were invariably helped, comforted and in many cases saved by him from mortal peril.

The Last Escape

On 11 January 1945, a week after the fatal Arrow Cross raid, we were awakened once more and nearly collapsed with fright. More armed men. Another raid? We were being invaded again, lights were shone in our faces, we were terrified, and then we looked more closely. This time it all seemed different. These men were not violent, they did not speak, and initially they just looked upon us with curiosity. Then we noted their faces. Asian? Chinese? Mongolian? And their clothes? Padded vests, heavy boots and a different type of helmets and earmuffs. Their weapons were primitive looking, with wooden handles, rather than the elegant, glistening, state-of-the-art, beautiful German Mausers, perfections of machine design.

No. These were not the accursed Nazis, the rotten cannibals of the twentieth century. These were the Russians, the Red Army! We had survived. We were liberated. We jumped up to kiss them, and then suddenly a volley of automatic fire rang out. The accursed SS was firing into our room from the building across the market gardens, but they missed us as we were standing kissing the Russians. We flattened ourselves as the Russians rushed out. Fighting ensued. A few hundred yards away, the Germans had converted a neighbouring hospital into an SS base. We were then hustled into the basement as the Russians went on to wipe out all the rotten Germans they could find. We were forever grateful for the Red Army for our liberation. May the Nazis be cursed forever.

Next morning, along the wall where I normally slept, we found the impact mark of the small-calibre German automatic machine gun and one of the actual bullets in our bedclothes, nickel or steel, 3.5cm long, and about 4mm in diameter.

I am not sure which of my eight close shaves was the most chilling, but one could have been enough. I do not know how to celebrate my escape. Instead I will just reflect. This year 2015 is the seventieth anniversary of my liberation by the Red Army. I keep thinking about that event. Time has not dimmed my acute feelings of joy and my hate for the Nazis who had terrorised us for years and taken such a toll. The fact that in the last seconds the SS fired at the room where we were kissing the Russians and missed me by a whisker perhaps heightens the emotional impact after seventy years.

Two depositions, reproduced in the Appendix at the end of this book, detail the fate that awaited us if we had not escaped the Arrow Cross checking our papers.

Chapter Four

MY PARENTS

My Mother

I was an only child, born in 1935, a year after the Nüremberg Laws were enacted, a bad time to have a large family. My mother, born in Budapest in 1909, was the second child of her parents. Her uncle, Imre Keve, was a chemical engineer who studied in Cambridge and spent two years in the US, where he contracted tuberculosis and died in 1933.

I have difficulty being clinical in describing my mother. She was slim, small, with hazel eyes and auburn hair, very bright without being intrusively chatty. At the age of seventeen she suffered a catastrophic X-ray-related burn to the right side of her chest and abdomen, which interrupted her studies. She was sent to Paris where she studied dressmaking, and after she returned she became a paediatric nurse and a radiology technician, later a secretary to the director of an institute. She spoke four languages fluently. She had a charismatic personality imbued with goodwill. An impossibly fortunate combination of all these qualities that I respect, including insight and an understanding of values that matter.

My mother and I had a very special relationship, and some months towards the end of her terminal illness in Australia I felt the world was coming to an end. I knew life would never be same after she had gone, but somehow, like all young people, I could not actually believe she was going to die. I knew that my life could be regarded as having essentially two phases, one while she was alive, and the rest, which really did not matter. I seriously contemplated suicide and felt absolutely devastated when the end came. But in a flash of insight I realised that I have been privileged and, without knowing it before that moment, I had the Supreme Being looking over me. Although I adored her, I could never show my affection sufficiently. Her cancer had to be treated psychologically as a matter of fact, and I felt showing my real concern might alarm her. With hindsight I wish we had discussed death more in line with the modern practice of openness, and to have shown her how I really felt.

There is an old proverb: 'God could not be everywhere, so he created mothers.' Nowhere does it apply more than in the case of a central European Jewish boy like myself, who lost his father to the Nazis, and who was sheltered, saved, educated, and brought out into the West by a single mother with no resources, and then given the chance to complete a university course, and the impetus to survive after the guardian angel had passed.

It is not appropriate to single out acts of insight, wisdom, courage, decisiveness, tenderness or any other actions in my mother's life. The mainstream was caring and goodwill, coupled with a degree of intelligence which I have encountered only in a very small number of other people. There is however a thread in her whole *Weltanschauung* which was consistent – she acted on her own judgment at all times. Like her son, she consulted friends and advisors, but never accepted any advice uncritically, and in the end she tended to follow her own uncanny intuition. My mother realised early in her life, quite in contrast to her family who incidentally comprised talented people, that Hungary offered no long-term future for a Jew. She wanted desperately to make me grow up in the West, especially after the Holocaust, and when the tragedy of our losses became apparent this became an overwhelming motive for her activities.

She had worked as a nurse, secretary, technician and economic director of a children's hospital, sometimes combining those jobs. She earned the usual pittance of a salary given to women in Europe – there were no allowances for children, holiday loadings, pensions, government subsidies, and so on. Jobs paid only a sometimes livable, sometimes barely livable, wage. On that salary she saved enough so that, after selling all our belongings and personal goods, she was able to hire a guide to help us escape to the West in 1949. Earlier than that, however, as early as 1945–1946, she sent some of our goods to Austria through people engaged in professional smuggling, who were often unreliable. She was desperately keen to assure a fundamental degree of security for us in case we were able to escape, with only our clothes on our backs, later that year. The smugglers got caught, the goods were lost, and we were lucky not to be arrested and persecuted for economic crimes against the socialist state: such charges were not uncommon.

Planning to Leave Hungary

Mother never invested hopes in any permanent existence in Hungary after the war. In contrast she gradually disposed of our furniture and a small piece of land, as well as the remnants of my grandparents' books, in order to have a degree of economic support later, when we became refugees. It was another tragedy that the nest egg she built up was stolen by distant relatives now living in Israel, who were entrusted with my mother's handbag before we reached Vienna, and who never returned it to us. They had travelled on the same train as us, but with a legitimate passport, while we were illegal escapees.

Much earlier my mother had trained as a nurse in anticipation of the hardships ahead. When, soon after my birth, Hungary's first Jewish laws were enacted, my father lost his job because of them. He never became permanently employed again and our standard of living had to adjust to the change. Later, when Father went absent without leave from his slave labour battalion to visit us, he was caught. My mother had the courage to go to the commanding officer, Colonel Murray, a rabid anti-Semite responsible for major war crimes in the Ukraine and subsequently hanged, to plead for my father and get him pardoned without serious punishment.

As soon as the Nazis controlled occupied Hungary my mother knew we were doomed. Many others in my family – magnates, intellectuals, bankers and businessmen – were stupefied as though drugged: 'It cannot happen to us. We are Hungarian citizens. What happened in Eastern Europe is different. They fought against Germany. We are allies!' My mother knew better and harboured no illusions.

Although financially impoverished and thus not able to escape, my mother made plans for hiding me, which were quite complex and imaginative. I was to pass myself off as the illegitimate son of an Aryan midwife in her hospital. After procuring these false papers and identity, I could have been hidden in a village as an orphan, a victim of bombing raids, or I could have gone underground with her at short notice at a later date. My false name was Raile Endre Kálmán László, not too difficult to remember, but I could not describe, even if compelled, my supposed place of birth. Naturally I was consulted and there was ever only one option: stay together. This option was always paramount, and even when taken to be executed and luckily rescued by Wallenberg, the fear of dying was more than compensated for by the presence of my mother.

In Russian villages and in the Baltic States, stories abound of whole villages being exterminated by the *Einsatzgruppen* in a few hours, in a totally matter-of-fact, premeditated, elegant, precise manner. Always there were one or two survivors not caught in the first wave, who watched or heard the executions and then meekly reported to be slaughtered, not wanting to abandon their loved ones. I could always identify with such people.

My mother was among the first to apply for permission to live in a hospital which was under the nominal protection of the neutral nations, and being a competent worker and a friend of the administration, she was allowed to move in there with me. This move was precipitated because our own apartment was requisitioned at twenty-four hours' notice by the Hungarian Ministry of the Interior to house some gentile bombing victims of allied raids. The 'victims' turned out to be the sister of the flat's caretaker, who reported that there were Jews living in the house, and demanded that their flat be surrendered to the caretaker's relatives. We did not know this and gave the caretakers a lot of tinned foods and asked them to look after our flat. After Liberation my mother returned to the building and demanded the flat back. She had all the contents returned and subsequently disposed of everything. The occupiers fled to Germany and, being Nazi sympathisers, justly feared retribution.

Immediately after the war, Mother suggested I start learning English, an idea I readily embraced. She spoke it well and was able to converse in English with the Russian Military Commander of Budapest when his children were having their tonsils removed at the same time as I had mine operated on. The Commander's children and I were in the same ward, and I remember my mother vividly chatting with the Russians in a language I never heard before. I was just nine years old, and learning English was the first great freedom she conferred on me. The second was escaping to the West. The third freedom was the vocation of medicine, a choice made in 1949 but a logical one given our family's background, my mother's nursing past, and our living in a hospital in 1944–1945. It was a choice I am glad to have made, but it certainly was made at great personal sacrifice by Mother, who was forty years old at that stage. With four to five years of high school and about six years of university ahead of me, it would be a minimum of eleven years before I would be able to financially stand on my own feet. She thus made a conscious decision to support me, in a type of nursing job in a foreign country, with minimum support from anyone, for eleven years, under the unremitting pressure of my study.

If only her health had stood up, she would have been very happy to see me graduate and would have felt it was well worth it, but given the eventual tragedy of her illness, I wish we could have acted differently, and that I had spent more time making her last months more tolerable. But there were many highlights in her life – Mother had a personality which was able to combine kindness and intelligence, not a combination readily given to many people. Her life was a blessing, and I mourn her illness and passing away as intensely now as when she left me.

The Vajda Family

My father Lászlo Vajda was born on 14 April 1907 in a part of Transylvania which is currently part of Romania. In that region there is a small hamlet, the village of Vajda, a name common in the Polish language, although spelt with a 'w'; in Hungarian it means a gipsy chieftain. The village is close to Marosvásárhely – 'Targu Mures' in Romanian – where this story begins. A well-known Prime Minister of Romania in the early part of the twentieth century answered to the name of Vajda-Vojvod. It was from the name of this village of Vajda that Zsigmond Weiss, my grandfather, changed his name to a Hungarian surname. It was a practice common in those early years of the century, when the emancipation of Jews in civil law, although not acknowledged by the religious authorities, was gradually taking place.

My paternal grandfather, Zsigmond Vajda, was born in about 1880 in Karcag. He was a book-keeper, with a quiet, self-effacing personality. He died in May 1944, tragically at the time when the deportations to Auschwitz were beginning, and my father, who attended his funeral, was caught on the train and deported. My paternal grandmother was a stunning-looking, dark haired, strong lady. Born around 1880, Rózsa Mendelssohn was from Marosvásárhely in Transylvania, where my father and uncle also lived. During the Holocaust period my mother arranged for Rózsa to be admitted to the hospital where she and I sheltered, and Rózsa survived the siege, atrocities and starvation. But Rózsa was devastated at the failure of her two children to return from the war, and died in mid-1945, possibly having committed suicide.

My grandmother Anna Weiss, who was born in what is now Slovakia, was also linguistically gifted and widely read. She was pivotal early on in my education, as my parents had to go to work. She had two brothers, János Weiss and Nándor Weiss, who managed to run the family stationery business until the Depression, when they lost it all. Both died in the early 1940s. Nándor and his wife Nellie had one son, who perished in the Ukraine, murdered in Dorosics by their Hungarian military guards. János Weiss and Margit Wilde had one son, Ferenc, known as Feri, who was born in 1914, survived and died in Budapest in 2000. Margit was a victim of an Arrow Cross massacre of thirty-five hospital patients, shot in the Danube on 3 January 1945, while we were hiding.

My grandparents had two sons: Andor, always referred to as Bandi, and Lászlo, my father, four years younger, nicknamed Laci. Both were born in Marosvásárhely, a large commercial centre, having equally large Romanian and Hungarian populations, augmented by a sizeable Jewish community. The two boys were vastly different. Bandi, tall and elegant, was an observant Jew who put on the phylacteries each morning on weekdays and prayed solemnly. He was a witty, cynical intellectual, and years later his comments became bywords in the family. 'He is not as big as his cousins, but twice as smart', he said of me. This was the most flattering compliment I had ever received. How could I forget it, or even fail to mention it?

Although he was always surrounded by ladies, Bandi never married and had no children. He doted on me and unquestionably became my favourite relative and a role model for me at the age of four or five, when children are obsessed by 'favourite' people, toys or activities. Bandi was a lover of art; he adored classical music, played the violin beautifully, and instilled in me a love for that instrument. He had a gramophone, an instrument not possessed by everyone at that period. He collected books in many languages, including Japanese art books on rice paper, the like of which I have not seen to this day. He loved classical writers – I remember his collection of rare books, such as the works of Villon, and translations of Villon by the legendary poet laureate and writer George Faludy, whom I had the fortune to meet in Canada sixty years later. Bandi spoke many languages, and had even been to Vienna and Italy, which in those days was an uncommon extravagance for a family with just one modest wage.

The Vajda family moved to Budapest around the time of the outbreak of the First World War, partly I suspect because of the danger of living in an area continually disputed between Romania and Hungary, and partly as a result of better job prospects in the bustling, cosmopolitan capital of Hungary, with its large, Jewish, middle-class population, and flourishing commerce and industry.

The most frequently asked question people put to me as a very young boy was 'What are you going to do when you grow up?' Invariably I replied: 'I will become an architect like Bandi'. He did become an architect, graduating from the Budapest Technical University, no mean feat in a period of increasing discrimination and at the cost of financial sacrifice, achieved by the family living more than modestly for many years. The problems of financial hardship did not end with his graduation, attested by a beautiful diploma (which is one of my very scant remaining heirlooms), because the collapse of the stock market in 1929 and the resulting Great Depression provided very few job opportunities, and within two years the ugly menace of Hitler was firmly resonating in Germany. It was obvious soon enough that I was not going to be architect, as I had no skill at drawing, I did not think in spatial terms, and as much as I had liked to handle Bandi's pencils and sets of compasses, or buy new sets of coloured crayons, I had not shown the least talent for expressing ideas graphically.

My Father

My father was a tall, good-looking man, with a likeable personality and keen intellect, but less successful academically than Bandi. He matriculated and entered university to study economics, but had to drop out as a result of financial hardship – his parents could not afford to send two boys to university – combined with regular confrontations with bands of anti-Semitic youths who frequently entered classes and beat up Jews. This diminished the incentive to continue with tertiary studies, and my father had no assured future at the end of the road in any case. He worked in the Manfréd Weiss works as an office employee, and later tried to make a living after he was forced to give up his job. Father was not observant, he did not play music, he could not speak foreign languages – except German, which hardly counts – and did not have enough money to collect books, or anything for that matter, at any period in his life. He was just a lovely, kind and humane person who had the insight to know the world was cruel but not sufficient insight to become ruthless enough in trying to save himself.

Around 1930, Bandi met a girl whose father was a surgeon from a wealthy family about to be ruined by the Depression. I understand Bandi was very taken with her, but soon afterward Laci, my father, moved in and won the girl – my mother – marrying her in the Dohány utca Synagogue, an ornate building, still in existence, the largest temple in Eastern Europe. The wedding photo, which survives only in my memory, depicts about forty-five people outside the Shul in the customary, ornate, elegant dress of the era, with hats and feathers for the ladies.

My parents loved rowing, and often hired skiffs to go on excursions along the Danube, pausing among the scattered little islands along the way. Bandi was an avid photographer and had a Rolleiflex camera, a rare luxury, to keep mementoes of these excursions. He had a habit of taking innumerable shots of me in special situations, such as sitting in the bath, playing in the park, riding a pony or sailing a toy boat on a lake. Miraculously many of these photos have survived.

One day I recall Father bought me a birthday present of a wire-controlled toy car. I threw a tantrum because that was not precisely the car I wanted: 'Take that rubbish away. I want the Schuko toy sports car, which has a horn, a steering wheel and a clutch, I won't have this wire-controlled rubbish', I sobbed. Next day the Schuko toy car arrived; Bandi had bought it for me, I suspect at enormous cost, and I have had a lasting feeling of guilt and self-reproach for being offensive to my father in that way.

Persecution Begins

The Vajda grandparents lived on the Pest side of the river, and Bandi lived with them for both support and economy. Unfortunately, by the time I was able to form definite memories, Bandi was drafted for compulsory slave labour service; his return after a few weeks of service always caused indescribable joy. Father's turn to be called up came soon after; he was required to report to Alsódabas, a god-forsaken village, now memorable only as a collection point for Jewish men on the way to humiliation and eventual martyrdom.

Holding down jobs became as difficult as getting employment in the first place. The restrictive anti-Jewish laws, first introduced in 1938, caused a sizeable proportion of families to become impoverished. They limited the employment of Jews by firms, initially to five percent and later to one percent of the work force. This applied even to Jewish-owned companies. One of my mother's relatives, who was the managing director of the Globus canning works, helped my father get a job at Manfréd Weiss, in the food processing division. After the passing of hostile legislation, Father was repeatedly passed over for promotion, and had to endure problems of discrimination and political opposition in keeping his job. He became very bitterly disillusioned and would not go to work. I remember bitter arguments, and Mother's persuasion to try to convince him to swallow his pride. It was a trying, soul-destroying situation, which ended with the outbreak of war, when he was dismissed and drafted for permanent slave labour.

Both Father and Bandi were short-sighted and wore glasses. They both recognised that this made them vulnerable because the guards picked on 'filthy Jewish intellectuals' – Nazi indoctrination focused on physical frailties of this sort. Consequently Father stopped wearing glasses, as occasionally they were knocked off from his face and head by brutal Hungarian soldiers guarding the battalions of slave labourers. 'The bastards stole my trench coat', he said mournfully on one occasion. The best articles of clothing, pens, pocket knives, watches, or any article a guard fancied, were was just physically grabbed, often with an added beating to show the guard's appreciation. 'It is better to give them or even offer them something they would like, in order to get them off your back', my father used to say.

Off to War

When Hungary, a great European power, declared war on the 'feeble' Soviet Union, our family was suddenly summoned to a village in the country to say goodbye to Bandi. We went by train and had lunch in the shade of a tree on a farm. Bandi was thin, tired and badly dressed in his own civilian clothes, but with a military style army cap. According to regulations, the Hungarian State emblem, braid and buttons had been removed, so as to not let the filthy Jews desecrate these important symbols of Greater Hungary. There was a traditional well in the courtyard of the farm, with a T-shaped pole balancing the buckets used for fetching water. Pigs were grunting in the pigsties and the whole scene was typical country life. It is the first time I have seen such a place and it is indelibly imprinted in my memory.

Suddenly two soldiers appeared: 'Are you ready? Say goodbye', they ordered Bandi. He stood up, saluted, embraced his mother and the rest of his family, kissed me and marched away in a formal manner. It was only then that I understood the purpose of our visit. A special permission was granted to families of the labourers to say farewell prior to their battalion leaving for the front. This was in 1941. We never saw Bandi again. One forced labourer who survived tells the story of digging at some riverbank, under supervision of Nazi guards, when he heard whistling coming from the direction of a fellow labourer. He recognised the melody as a piece from the Brahms Violin Concerto. It was Bandi, whistling, and they became friends for life.

When Father's turn to be called up came soon he was to report to his battalion and was taken to Transylvania with his unit, where they were engaged in building fortifications. Fortunately at that time they were not sent to the Ukraine, a tragic country, the site of the extensive genocide for the slave labourers from Hungary and a graveyard for its own Jewish population.

There was no income for either my parents or my grandparents. Savings were almost non-existent. Even though there were no ghettoes, the Jewish population was under constant economic and thinly-veiled physical threats. My mother enrolled to become a nurse in order to have a profession. She spoke four languages, French and English as well as Hungarian and German, and was a dressmaker, but she needed something more tangible. Father came home on leave on rare occasions, and on one of these periods my parents discussed the possibility of his escaping from the slave labour battalion and going over to the Russians. 'The problem is that the Russians are still too far away, I don't know the terrain, even though I was born there', he would say of Transylvania. 'Besides, I wouldn't know what sort of reception we would get from the Russians.' It was rumoured that the Russian troops could not, or would not, make a distinction between Jewish slaves and their bitter enemies, the Fascist fighting troops, and it was feared that all would be treated equally abysmally. Father believed it would still be an improvement to being a slave under the boots of our own brutal guards, totally exposed to every sadistic whim of the moment. He told stories, which I was not allowed to hear, of the torture and decimation of young men thrown at the guards' mercy.

The war turned in the Russians' favour. The Germans occupied Hungary. Accompanying the Wehrmacht was the Eichmann *Sondereinsatz Kommando*, with their experienced butchers, their hands stained with the blood of four million European Jews already slaughtered. The date was 19 March 1944. Within weeks the country was to be cleansed of Jews. Blueprints for genocide were all carefully prepared in the drawers of the offices of Endre and Baky, Secretaries of State for Jewish Affairs.

Life in Budapest

My maternal grandmother died on April 21. At the funeral the arrest of Jews was imminent, and our demise was avoided only by a timely air-raid. My grandfather Zsigmond died on May 10. By this time it was positively dangerous to go to the funeral, but my parents attended nevertheless. Father was given special leave for that purpose. As he explained: 'It was not kindness that made the Army grant me leave to go the funeral – they had an ulterior motive. The battalion commander knew I used to work in the food industry and ordered me to get a consignment of tinned food for the officers, as they were running short of supplies at the front.' The date of this leave period was ominous – the deportations were scheduled to begin on 15 May 1944, starting with the eastern part of Hungary.

There was a total ban on Jews using the railways. This was enforced not by the railway authorities, but by periodic checks on travellers carried out by the gendarmes, soon to become notorious as the Hungarian equivalent of the SS. Father came home from the funeral to say goodbye. I was playing on the floor. 'Are you not going to get up to say goodbye to your father?' my mother asked. I had not seen him come in. We said farewell and he kissed me in front of the mirror of the cupboard in the front room of the house, and I have retained that moment in my memory for the rest of my life. I have thought long and deep about this moment, and remember his face and touch and features and warmth. I lost him that day, and by losing him I lost what was left of my childhood.

The war, deportations, eviction from our home, and relocation to a 'Jewish house', followed one after another in a relatively rapid sequence over the next few months. By July 1944 the death machinery for the Jews of Hungary had been well tested and found effective. The countryside had become *Judenrein* (cleansed of Jews) and it was Budapest's turn. We lost our apartment and, as I have related above, moved into the Alice Weiss Hospital for women, where my mother was employed and which through a quirk of fate had become a diplomatically 'protected house'. Mother was employed to be secretary to the Director, and in addition one morning each week she was on duty at the front desk, marked 'Information', near the front gate of the hospital.

Rumours abounded about the imminent start to the deportations and everybody was jittery and hatching plans as best they could to try to escape the trains to Auschwitz. A man in civilian clothes arrived at the front desk and asked for my mother by name. We were naturally very apprehensive. The stranger asked outright: 'What happened to your husband? Are you hiding him? Where is he hiding? Did he escape from the army deliberately? Do you know what the punishment for escape is? This is wartime, you could all be shot.' My mother explained all the circumstances in detail, stating that Father left eight weeks before to rejoin his unit in Transylvania on 12 May 1944, the day after his father's funeral. She explained: He had an official warrant to travel by train, signed by the battalion commander. He arranged food for the officers in the battalion, a fact which could be verified, and he did not delay even by one day. He left on a train departing from the Eastern railway station at 4pm that day.'Can you give us any information about what could have happened to him, if he has not returned to the army unit?' my mother enquired.

The detective, obviously employed by army intelligence, remained noncommittal, but did not force the issue. He appeared to believe my mother, because the explanation was already suspected and because similar stories occurred very often indeed. The explanation was not a mystery to the authorities, but the army still went through the routine of confirming what had happened. He insisted on interrogating me separately (I was eight years old at the time) and thus obtained confirmation of Mother's story. This seemed to satisfy him and he left. I recall to this day the double feeling of relief after this episode. First the selfish relief that they were not persecuting Mother and myself, and secondly a vague but quietly jubilant feeling that maybe Father had escaped and, as agreed at his last visit in discussion with my mother, possibly managed to go over to the Russians. For many years later I still had that gnawing doubt, in spite of all the later eyewitness evidence and documentary proof to the contrary, that perhaps our later information was incorrect and, hope against hope, maybe Father managed to escape. A pipedream, long ago extinguished.

One day a letter arrived from the Ministry of Defence stating that Lászlo Vajda, Jewish labour serviceman, was removed by members of the Gendarmerie Training Battalion from a passenger train during the return trip to his unit in Transylvania. He was delivered to the ghetto of Oradea (also known as Nagyvárad), and his further destination was unknown. The Army was not going to divulge that he had been deported to the gas chambers at Auschwitz, together with 30,000 members of the Oradea Jewish community. This was one tangible result of the annexation of Northern Transylvania by Hungarian troops in 1940, and the occupation of Hungary by Hitler in 1944. How could the world, and in particular German civilians, claim to have been ignorant of mass murder in Nazi occupied territories, when in July 1944, I, although a child, knew from stories being circulated by word of mouth, about lime pits, gas chambers and showers, into which people were crammed to suffocate them?

Chapter Five

THE FATE OF MY FATHER

Searching for Father

I never seriously experienced starvation, as my mother always saved food for me. Rumours of the murder of children, attacks on hospitals, surrender of children hidden by nuns, deportations on foot, threats to burn the ghetto, created an atmosphere of all pervasive horror, accompanied by viciousness and threats. Then a second attack on us took place, the murder of my schoolteacher, friends, and relatives with whom we shared a room, and finally Liberation in 1945.

I recall getting a registered airmail letter from Paris in 1946, which was addressed to me and for a brief moment raised my hopes – perhaps it was from Father or maybe from Bandi. But it was not to be. It was merely a school friend whose family had escaped to the West, writing to say they had arrived. What a total disappointment. I threw away the letter and never replied. Later, in 1949, we left Hungary, a land which had treated us so brutally. We had not heard from my father. We were still hopeful that maybe he had escaped toward the end of the war, but this hope grew fainter as each year passed.

After we left Hungary my mother and I stayed for eighteen months in a *Flüuchtlingslager* (refugee camp) in Steyr, upper Austria. Mother worked in the camp as a nurse and thus received a pittance and some privacy of accommodation. Card playing was a popular way to pass the interminable waiting for the interviews, permits, medicals and bureaucratic hurdles each refugee had to surmount. In Steyr one day in 1949 Mother was invited by a group of friends to play bridge. She introduced herself to another new member of the group: 'Vajda Lászlóné'. The man she addressed looked up, electrified: 'What did you say your name was?' Mother was alerted. She repeated her name, which according to custom used her husband's first name, preceded by the equivalent of 'Mrs'. 'Would you have a photo of your husband? Or is he with you?' Ligeti enquired. 'He disappeared in 1944', said Mother. 'According to our last information he was taken off the train as a labour serviceman and attached to the Nagyvárad ghetto. I have not heard any more from him.' The man – George Ligeti – slowly replied: 'Vajda László was my best friend in the Nagyvárad ghetto, in the cattle truck to Auschwitz, in the death march to Mauthausen, and we were together in Ebensee, that horrible camp where virtually nobody survived. He died of starvation in Ebensee a few weeks before it was liberated by the Americans.' What else was there to add?

I was in Graz in Austria at the time, going to school, learning another language. I visited Mother at the camp in Steyr at every possible opportunity. On my visit at the end of 1949 she told me this story, and would not elaborate. Nor did I ask her to. I could not bear talking about it, nor talking with Ligeti, who became a friend and finally settled in the town we migrated to, two years later. For thirty-five years I kept my distance from Ligeti, and never revived the past. By that time, 1985, I had made many statements, television and public appearances about Wallenberg.

Learning the Truth

One day I met George Ligeti in the street. 'How are you? Nice to see you,' he said, 'We must have a long chat one day.' I nodded. I did not want to tell him that even forty years after my father's disappearance, the thought of finding out how he was murdered was far too much to bear. He paused for a moment, as though he had understood. 'I followed your stand on Wallenberg', he said slowly, 'I thoroughly approve. There is one thing, though. I do not want you to say ever again that you would be happiest if Wallenberg were released, more than anyone else, even your father. Never say that again. Your father to me was like Wallenberg.'

And he told the story: 'We were taken off the passenger train, *en route* to re-joining our labour units, at Nagyvárad. The cruel gendarmes took off all Jews, whether slave labourers or civilians, and forced them under armed guard to march to the grossly overcrowded ghetto, the biggest in provincial Hungary. Thirty thousand people were locked up under conditions of appalling severity, with overcrowding and lack of facilities. A group of the wealthier people were cruelly tortured to discover where their valuables were hidden. The pejorative name for the ghetto was 'the mint', because the Hungarian authorities were beating the money out of their captives. After ten days of hell, during which suicides and deaths were common, and the first transport had already left, we were crammed into the same cattle truck as the observant Jews of Nagyvárad. There were two wagons holding the labour servicemen. As usual the wagons were filled to the extreme, no room to sit or lie, and virtually no sanitation or water.

'In the cattle truck the religious Jews were using the water – one bucket for eighty people – to wash their hands before prayers, instead of quenching their thirst. Conditions were indescribably horrible. We were fit, so we survived that journey, but many did not. In the cattle wagon in front of us, some of the servicemen cut away the floor or the side of the wooden structure. At night, when the guards were not so alert, about half of them escaped.' (What a tragedy that my father was not in the first wagon, but in the one following, as he could have also escaped, especially as he had already made plans for such an eventuality.) 'We talked about escaping', George went on. 'We could have done it. We had the means to cut the floor, but we did not do so. Do you know why? Because we were afraid of collective punishment meted out for those who would have been left behind. The gendarmes had threatened us that if anyone escaped, the rest would be punished. We did not know where we were being taken. We knew nothing of Auschwitz. This was May fifteenth. The process had just started.

'A week before that, we had been labouring in the Transylvanian forests near Dédabisztra. Who could have guessed what was to happen to the deportees? So we stayed. Nothing special happened to those in the other wagon who stayed behind. What could have happened? They were selected, some to die at once, some to be worked to death like us, no one knew who came from where. Eighty percent were sent straight to the gas chambers. Our group of about sixty people were all fit, strong men of military age, toughened by erecting fortifications prior to our arrest. We marched into Auschwitz as a military unit, and reported, in German, to Mengele, the infamous murderer carrying out a "selection": "Sir, the Hungarian auxiliary labour service battalion wishes to report for work." We were all spared to work, and your father was subsequently allotted to the Kanada Kommando, employed to empty the trains of the victims' belongings. The owners by this time were being turned into smoke and ashes. There were opportunities working in the Kommando to organise and hide valuables and scraps of food, so that both of us managed to survive Auschwitz,' George continued.

I had visions of my father sorting out piles of clothes for children and wondering with inner horror when the Budapest Jews, including his son, would arrive, and whether he would be able to catch a last glimpse of me before I was sent to the gas chamber, as I would certainly be murdered, being only eight years old, well below an age where there was a possibility of survival, nor being a twin who had 'experimental' value.

Father and Ligeti remained in Auschwitz until 17 December 1944, when the SS declared that the camp was to be evacuated to prevent prisoners from falling into Russian hands. The prisoners debated vigorously whether to stay or to follow orders and join the evacuation. In the end they decided to obey; another fatal decision. They judged it safer to leave with their tormentors, as there was a real risk of the camp being set alight, and those staying being burnt alive. This was the usual precedent. The dawn of departure had arrived.

Ligeti continued: 'Suddenly I see your father coming to me, running. He is carrying a large shoe-box, full of lump sugar. He hands it to me with the following words: "Take this George, it's some food, distribute it among the boys", adding quietly: "Who knows when we will see food again?"' This was the last time George saw my father in Auschwitz. My father, who gave away a shoebox full of sugar to help his friends after spending six months in Auschwitz, did not survive. He was starved to death. George survived. I understood what George meant about humanity. My father was starved to death in the Mauthausen sub-camp of Ebensee, on 7 March 1945, eight weeks before the Liberation.

Memories of Lupa Island

At a later meeting Ligeti recalled that the misery of Auschwitz was hardly ever relieved by anything from outside. The endless transports, the daily arrival of innocents to the slaughter, the selections, the misery of slave labour, the lack of food, the constant fear of death, and the ever-present spectacle of degradation all contributed to the feeling of doom, the trampling of the human soul underfoot. One of the ways of trying to remain human was to speak of the happier past, especially of loved ones and times when a Jew was still regarded as a human being, who had friends, a home and was able to enjoy what people have always taken for granted: the right to live.

Forty years later, when I spoke to George about his time in the Lager, he recalled reminiscing about happier times with my father, whilst suffering in the hell of Auschwitz. My father would tell him stories, of which one about Lupa Island remained a cherished event, not only in my father's memory in 1944, but also in Ligeti's memory in 1984. Lupa Island is an oasis in the Danube near Budapest, where my father had spent occasional happy hours on holidays, and where he enjoyed a break from the stress of trying to make a living in a harsh, unforgiving world, increasingly racist and intolerant.

I remember Father saying to me one day: 'Get dressed, we are going on a day trip. We'll go fishing, swim in the Danube, and my friends have some pets – you'll enjoy it.' Because such memories are, sadly, all too few, they are treasured even more acutely. So that morning we set out by tram and local train to Lupa Island. Our friends had a small house, a boat and a ramp leading to the water to launch it. They had two, small, wire-haired terriers. I was a city boy, we never had pets as they could not be kept inside, nor could we afford them and even the laws of tenancy prohibited keeping animals. Thus until I became much older – I was six years old at this time – I did not even know the different breeds of dogs. 'What type of dogs are they? What model?' I asked, thinking of cars, probably. 'Terriers' was the answer, 'they make a lot of noise, but are quite intelligent and won't bite you'. I was reassured and became very friendly with them. These were the first dogs I ever played with or really got to know by name.

We went rowing and I was to act as the cox, but of course there were some problems. I could not understand that I had to pull the rope in the direction opposite to where we wanted to go. So I was constantly helped by Father and my efforts caused a lot of amusement amongst the adults. After lunch there was my first ever attempt at fishing. I was standing on the ramp, holding a rod with a line. Father was in the water, and suddenly I fell in. He swam to me, and picked me out (I could not swim), warned me about ever getting too close to the edge, at least until I became safe in the water. It is hard to believe that this visit to a holiday resort left such a vivid memory, with my first animals, rowing and fishing, all linked to this rare treat of an excursion. Etching the essentials of this minor incident is another memorial to happier times, which had been keenly appreciated by all three of us.

The Mauthausen Death List

The first time I met the Nazi hunter Simon Wiesenthal, the man after whom my son is named, we spoke about Mauthausen and the various sub-camps he knew, and of my mother's attempts to locate the site where my father was likely buried. In Wiesenthal's opinion, Father was probably cremated, a view in accord with the records of the *Standesamt Gemeinde Mauthausen* (Mauthausen civil registration office), which contains a list of victims, largely of Jewish slave labourers from Hungary who were killed in the camp, a list drawn up at the request of the American occupation forces. It remained unpublished until 1990, when it appeared in full in a book by Professor Szita Szabolcs, a Hungarian historian who over the past thirty years had delved deeply into the fate of the Jewish deportees.

At the time of the fiftieth anniversary of the Holocaust in Hungary, 1944 to 1994, I organised an exhibition and memorial service at the Holocaust Museum in Melbourne, selecting many exhibits, based on photographs and historical documents, with the *Auschwitz Album* as its centrepiece. During the preparations I was loaned a book entitled *The Journey Back from Hell: Memoirs of a Concentration Camp Survivor*. In that book, which I used largely for its photographic content, there was an appendix. With the exhibition over, and with the emotions and distress associated with remembrance slowly subsiding, I decided to return the book. Before returning it I glanced through the appendix, which contained a list of names. Among the 7000 victims of Mauthausen there was the name, birthplace, birthdate, and date of death of my father.

Austria, Mauthausen/Gusen Concentration Camp Death Record Books, 1938–1945, about Ladislaus Vajda

Name:	Ladislaus Vajda
Birth Date:	14 Apr 1907
Birth Place:	Marosvásárhely
Mauthaus #:	119397
Nationality:	Ungarn (Hungary)
Arrest Reason:	Jude (Jew)
Night and Fog:	No
Profession:	Seifensieder (Soap Boiler)
Death Date:	7 Mar 1945
Death Place:	Zement (Ebensee)
Arrival Date:	25 Jan 1945

I still find this too horrifying to contemplate or even to comment on.

Jacob Rosenberg

Another survivor of Ebensee, Jacob Rosenberg, became my dear friend for twenty years until his passing. He was a wonderfully wise and gentle writer, and a man of the highest standards. I met him after I launched a book on the Holocaust in Hungary, during which I had spoken of the tragic fate of adult males during this period, and of my father murdered in Ebensee. Ebensee was a sub-camp of Mauthausen and the most brutal; only a tiny percentage of people survived the terrible deprivations, cold, hunger, sadism, and disease. Jacob came up to me after the book launch and quietly said: 'I survived Auschwitz and Ebensee'. A dramatic meeting.

Jacob was about seventy when we met. Born in Lodz in Poland, he lost fifty members of his family in the Shoah. Like many of us he was haunted by images of his broken life and murdered family. The common bond between Jacob and my father's friend George Ligeti was that both had experienced Auschwitz, passed through Mauthausen, and were liberated at Ebensee. Coming from an observant family Jacob was a student of the Talmud, and spoke Yiddish as his native tongue. Although his outlook and philosophy were altered dramatically after the Holocaust, he remained the archetypal Jew, a lover of his people who had an abiding interest in Israel, read avidly and was highly knowledgeable on Jewish and international affairs. Jacob had two most distinguishing characteristics. He was an accomplished writer, generating sonnets and other forms of poetry, as well as plays and elegies. These express, with the strictest economy of words, his insights and his sadness and anger at this world. Secondly Jacob was a man of kindness and compassion, a man not given to superficial vainglory, or ostentation in word or thought.

I took great care in selecting the people I introduced to Jacob. George, who suffered the same configuration of horror as Jacob, might have been thought to be a suitable companion to meet him, but there were significant differences in outlook between them. Jacob was a Jew, George is also of Jewish origin – Jewish enough for Nazi racism – but he is a convert, non-Jewish in his thinking and attitudes, and reluctant to identify with Jewish concerns which he has never been exposed to, or feels it necessary to be aware of.

There are many different attitudes among Jews. Some observant Jews who were fortunate enough to escape before 1939 have remained relatively unaltered after the Holocaust. On the other hand, many formerly observant Jews have partly abandoned its religious trimmings, frequently transferring their allegiance to Israel, which has become their God and can do no wrong. These people follow blindly the current Israeli thinking on any issue, and although not religious they still pay close attention to their former religious restrictions, having removed only some prohibitions on diet and matters of observance. Others have abandoned religion totally, and while not supporting Israel blindly they take part in some Jewish affairs, and certainly take a stand in the fight against Fascism and revisionist views of history. Another group takes no part in anything to do with Jews or Judaism, but do not deny their origin. Finally there are those who try to keep their children ignorant of their Jewish roots, often converting and educating their children to be actively non-Jewish.

Jacob was an educated, non-religious Jew, who did not abandon the ethics of religion. He was a strong but not blind supporter of Israel who certainly took a prominent part in the fight against Fascism. George on the other hand is a person who has no truck with Jewishness, although he does not deny his origins. The differences in attitude of these two people – who were treated with equal bestiality by the Nazis – would have made them difficult company for each other. Each has had the right to determine how to lead life after rebirth from the horrors of persecution. It may have been hoped that such different people may become at least acceptable to each other, but the risk was that they may not. This is why I could not take George Ligeti to the house of Jacob.

Jacob and I had many common bonds, the strongest of which was that we 'never forget and never forgive'. This is a phrase I used at a Yom HaShoah (Holocaust Remembrance Day) commemoration ceremony in 1994. Since then it has become repeated in print many times. Even if not closing our eyes to the horrors or drawing a kind veil, I think it is easier to forgive for those who were uninvolved, but to seek to force forgiveness on survivors is irrational.

Jacob told the story of his liberation from Ebensee:

'There were two facts that stand out. The Polish prisoners wanted to kill all the Jews who were still alive, a pitifully small number. They planned to murder them just before the Americans arrived and blame it on the Germans. When asked why, they replied: "The Jews will cause trouble, they will complain, accuse us and it is easier to kill them all." To their eternal credit, it was the Dutch Christians, the political prisoners interned in this Mauthausen sub-camp who objected, and made the Poles desist from the mass murder of their fellow victims.

'When liberation came, the tortured prisoners, citizens from twenty nations, made flags to represent their countries. The Jews had no country. None of the others permitted Jewish prisoners to join their group to wait for Liberation. On the fifth day of May, 1945, a tank rumbled to the gate. For the past twenty-four hours a few hundred survivors had been in a state of excitement, although they were physically almost beyond caring. Hunger and disease had killed about ten thousand of them within the past two months, there was absolutely no food and the bestial concentration camp structure was functioning until the last day. Suddenly a few soldiers jumped off the tank. They rushed through the gate. They were Americans.

'Inside the camp the skeletons were lined up, as if by pre-arrangement. The Germans had fled. The Americans started shouting: 'We are Americans. We are a Jewish battalion from Brooklyn, we are looking for our brothers. Where are the Jews?' A handful of Jewish survivors staggered forward and cried. They had no flag of their own.'

It was exactly two months too late to save my Father.

Chapter Six

FOUR RELATED FAMILIES

The Falus Family

My cousin Feri was the only son of uncle John on my grandmother's side. He was about eighteen years older than me, and remained one of my mentors during my upbringing. He had a good start in life. When he was born, at the time of the outbreak of World War One, his family had a comfortable home in his grandfather's huge building in central Budapest, which served as a wholesale stationery store. It has also served as living quarters for my maternal great grandfather Jakab's three children, the youngest of whom was Feri's father. All the children got married and had numerous children who were brought up, in the manner of that era, as a close and extended family.

Feri was a good-looking boy, with long, blond curly hair. He was a member of a Boy Scout group, and one of his most treasured memories was attending the World Scout Jamboree held in Hungary in August 1933, where he met scouts of other nationalities and made practical use of the three languages he spoke by the time he was sixteen. As the family belonged to so-called 'neolog' reform Jews who favoured integration, many had a good knowledge of German, largely fostered by having *Fräuleins* employed to care for children at an early age. These au pair girls managed to teach German to the children in the family, so that some spoke German as well their native tongue. Additionally, Feri quickly learned to speak English. This was aided by visits by his American relatives, who had emigrated at the turn of the century, prospered and returned time after time to renew old family ties.

Feri's mother, Margit, was the aunt of Kornél Wild, who made a film career in Hollywood. After changing his name to Cornel Wilde, he became a swashbuckling film star hero of popular B-grade movies. Cornel had studied medicine, and was also an excellent fencer, available for selection in the US Olympic fencing team, but his film career took a priority over these pursuits.

An interesting anecdote concerning Cornel, often recalled by the family, was that he visited Budapest in the late thirties at a time when anti-Semitism, having official support, was particularly rampant in Hungary. Many sporting clubs practiced racial discrimination, with Jews excluded from membership, and even being forbidden to enter club premises. Cornel Wilde was about to break the fast after Yom Kippur, when the phone rang: 'This is the MAC Fencing Club here, Count S.A. speaking, may I speak to Cornel Wilde, please?' The name did not augur well as the MAC club was a hub of Nazi sentiments. Cornel took the receiver: 'Hallo, this is Cornel Wilde', he said in perfect Hungarian. 'Welcome to Budapest, this is Count S.A., I would like to have the honour of inviting you to our weekly fencing exhibition at St. Margaret's Island tomorrow. May we have the pleasure of your company? All equipment and other costs are of course covered by the club.' 'What time tomorrow?' replied Cornel. 'Two o'clock in the afternoon, if that is convenient'. 'I'll be there' said the modest film star, and later explained to the family that he did not wish to keep conversing with this count for too long, because breaking the strict Day of Atonement fast was a serious business.

My dear cousin Feri was hoping to become a textile engineer. By the time he would have reached university, restrictions increasingly applied to Jewish students. The numerus clausus almost became the numerus nullus. The first anti-Jewish edict meant restricted entry to tertiary educational institutions, the second edict excluded Jews completely. Admiral Horthy, an admiral of a totally landlocked country, was the effective ruler of Hungary, with the title of Regent. He proudly told Hitler that he had started his anti-Jewish measures immediately after the First World War, long before any other European government, as he was fully able to recognise the menace of Jewish subversion of Aryan culture. Thus Feri never got beyond matriculation, but even that was a great achievement, and henceforth he was regarded as an 'educated man'.

By this time the Falus family was no longer affluent. In 1933, during the Depression, the family's fortune was wiped out, as stocks and shares plummeted. Feri's father and uncle, being decent and honest merchants, decided to honour all their creditors, and as a result they became destitute, as I have mentioned previously. It was far removed from their thinking to sign over assets and valuables to their wives or to accept bankruptcy as many competitors had done, only to resume trading afterwards. In those days bankruptcy was associated with a shameful stigma well beyond its current connotation.

The family business was heavily mortgaged because the sons liked to gamble on the stock exchange as well as on the horses.

The dark clouds of Hitlerism were gathering over the horizon. When Feri was in his twenties he was called up to compulsory labour service, a euphemism for slave labour and inhuman abuse. It was enthusiastically embraced by the Hungarian Fascists. Jewish boys were taken in their civilian clothes under the control of Nazi officers and frequently sadistic guards, forced to dig trenches, and work with a shovel and other precision instruments. After the entry of Hungary into the war in 1941, many of these battalions were taken to the eastern front where they suffered catastrophic losses, largely inflicted by the guards.

Feri was lucky. As far as I can recall, he never had to leave the country and was spared some of the horrors in the Ukraine. In 1944 while Feri was on leave in Budapest he visited us. I remember saying to him, pointing to a young lady who was staying with my parents as a guest for the weekend: 'Feri, let me introduce you to Ilu – she is my mother's best friend'. He married her within the week. Our lives henceforth were even more closely entwined. In August 1944 Feri suddenly reappeared from his slave labour conscription unit in the middle of the reign of terror, having escaped from the same Arrow Cross dominated military arsenal, the Albrecht Barracks, where earlier his wife, together with my mother and myself, had been taken for execution. After we were saved on that occasion, Feri joined us as a resident in the protected house, and no one asked questions. We shared the floor space of a small personnel office designed for four employees with twenty others.

Ilu, a talented office worker, was able to forge Swedish protection papers for a number of Jewish people who thereby escaped deportation. She recalled: 'There was a crowd of people at the Józsefvaros railway station, where the Jews were placed in cattle trucks. A gendarme officer was yelling "Bloody Jews, this paper is rubbish, it is not genuine, you are cheats. I'll show you what it's worth", and he tore up a genuine, highly valuable Swedish *Schutzpass* in the presence of the owner, whose fate was thereby sealed, condemned to deportation and death.' Ilu continued: 'My friend arrived next, carrying a passport I had fabricated. It was not only altered, but even before it had been changed to the name and personal details of the holder it was a false piece of paper to start with, because it had been printed by the Zionists, rather than by a neutral embassy. The gendarme, a member of the most viciously anti-Semitic group of scum, simply murderers who carried out the genocide in Hungary, then held up my forgery and proudly said: "This is what they should look like, this is a real passport, you can't hoodwink me", and he let the man go.'

Ilu and Feri were in the line-up when we were attacked in early January 1945 and Feri lost his mother, Margit, who ended her life on the banks of the Danube. Ilu lost her parents and a brother, who were deported to Auschwitz. Her sister married an ex-slave labourer, who was made to run across minefields in the Ukraine, and was maimed by a mine. He was totally blinded but was in the end, incredibly, repatriated and survived for many years.

We got on with living. We were liberated, but still starving. Meat appeared. We knew stories about horses falling and people scavenging them, but I was always told it was 'Wiener schnitzel'. People were so hungry that finding a bowl of cold beans was like striking gold; many adults would throw themselves at the bowl and devour the contents. Feri tried to make a living after Liberation, becoming a glazier. There were virtually no windows left intact in Budapest, but he could not obtain glass, as it had been strictly rationed out to the more influential firms. Eventually he took a job as a clerk.

Feri related a story that he was walking down the street with a friend who had lost his beautiful young wife in the Arrow Cross raids in January, when they suddenly saw a man, whom they both recognised. He was the Arrow Cross brigand who led the attack on the hospital. They jumped on him and nearly beat him to death, then took him to the police. The Arrow Cross man was locked up, and at his trial Feri had to undergo the trauma of recalling the events of the raid on that day. The key fact was that Feri said the man was brandishing an old World War One rifle, known as a Mannlicher, threatening the women and children with it. That was enough, as there were numerous witnesses, and there was no doubt about his participation in the event. He was hanged, or 'reached his death by the rope' as it is poetically expressed in his language.

A second trial followed. Another Arrow Cross officer was caught, and charged with numerous crimes. Feri was asked to give testimony that on one occasion this man had brought back Jews from execution, as he fancied one of the girls in the group. Feri said (and for this he has my full respect): 'I will not defend a murderer because he saved someone. If he killed a single person on another occasion, as he undoubtedly has done, he deserves to be punished.'

Two years after Liberation, Feri and I were passing through St. Stephen's park in Budapest where a statue to honour Raoul Wallenberg was erected, to be unveiled that day, but the ceremony was cancelled. Feri covered his mouth and leaned towards me: 'Of course you know of Raoul Wallenberg. He was the most wonderful man who helped us in Budapest to survive.' He then looked around suspiciously: 'You may not know, as you do not live in this district, but we subscribed the cost to erect a statue to honour him. Pál Pátzay, the doyen of Hungarian sculptors, created it, and the Wallenberg statue was set up here in preparation for the unveiling today.' He spoke even more softly: 'The Russians tore down the statue and dragged it away,' and he pointed to the base of the statue, which was still there. 'It is an absolute disgrace, but be very careful. Do not react, do not speak about it, there are secret police everywhere, especially around here.' I recall even now, fifty years later, the fear I experienced that day, looking behind the bushes, and thinking what a careless thing it was to speak about this in public, and what a tragedy it was that Wallenberg was taken by the Russians. Everybody knew that it was the Russians who took him. Thank the Lord, two years later we left my homeland, that site of mass murder.

We did not hear from Feri for the six or so years from the time we left Hungary in 1949 till 1956. We knew Ilu lost a number of babies; the ravages of war and her frail constitution did not help her to conceive. In 1956, after the Hungarian uprising, Ilu and Feri suddenly contacted me from Chile, of all places. A clever relative, who later distinguished himself by his total lack of care for Feri when he most needed it, later said about Feri's emigration and return: 'Why did he go? Why did he not tell anyone? Why Chile? And why did he come back to Hungary in the end?' Because Feri and Ilu did return to Hungary two years later.

The reason he left in the first place is not hard to understand. While most people were escaping from Communism, Feri and Ilu, who lost her parents and two brothers, had fears of a resurgence of anti-Semitism. They felt they could be a target. Who could blame them? To leave was a very intelligent decision; the choice of Chile was less so. But Ilu had a brother, Bandi, settled in Chile, so they felt they could count on some assistance.

Bandi had survived the Holocaust by a miracle. He was on a deportation train to Auschwitz, when the train, still in Hungary, stopped at a siding. Bandi remembered: 'The train stops and waits. Then another train arrives on the next siding. I look out the window. What's this? A long troop train with Hungarian soldiers. I raise myself to the barred window and look out, and would you believe it, facing me is a soldier whose face I recognise. It's my best friend from childhood, my comrade, my buddy. We had been inseparable for twenty years. I shout: "Lali! Can you hear me? It's me, Bandi. Get me out of here". Lali Bartfai takes six of his fully armed soldiers to escort him. He gets out of the train, walks up to the gendarmes who guard the human cargo on the way to extermination, and says: "This man is my half-brother. Let him out and we shall take him with us." The gendarmes frown: "You can't do that, he is a bloody Jew, we are taking him to the border to hand him over to the Germans. You can't have him." Lali Bartfai speaks softly: "Boys, weapons at the ready. Blast the heads off these fucking gendarmes." Some more soldiers appear and raise their guns. The brutal gendarmes, known for their brutality and merciless sadism rather than their bravery, retreat. "All right. Take him, but on your own responsibility."

By this time Bandi was out of the cattle truck and joining the army group. In speech he sounded like the archetypal Hungarian peasant and resembled the film star Alan Ladd in appearance. He survived.

Immediately after the war was over, Bandi escaped from Hungary and settled in Santiago, Chile, hence Feri's decision to immigrate to South America in the wake of the 1956 Hungarian uprising. Feri gave another reason for returning to Hungary: 'Uncle Eugene died. (Every Hungarian Jew has an uncle Eugene). I felt that my aunts in their eighties needed my support'. In the event Feri's aunties did not take kindly to their lost relative. Already they had had part of their flat requisitioned, and were forced to take in a sub-tenant. Then they committed the ultimate treason. They signed an agreement with these strangers that in exchange for being looked after in their old age; they bequeathed to them upon their death their nice flat in Budapest. Feri was mortified. He had problems getting employment, and had to appear before Communist Party investigation committees to justify his having escaped. He was eventually cleared and after living in penury, more by good luck than by good management he put a deposit on a superb dwelling overlooking Castle Hill in Buda, where he lived until his passing.

Ten years after the 1956 uprising we met in Slovakia. I was too apprehensive to enter Hungary, so we met outside the country. Subsequently we had numerous meetings, usually in Paris, Venice, Florence or Vienna. Feri received very bad medical treatment in Hungary, and died a very depressed man. He was a true gentleman and I am very lucky to have known him for many years.

After our meetings in Paris Feri realised my preoccupation with the Holocaust and procured for me countless volumes of hard-to-obtain literature, books, documents, videos, archive material and photocopies of out-of-print books for my library. He was able to do this largely as a result of his excellent contacts in libraries and in Jewish circles, where his old-world charm and kindness disarmed many of the dragons who tend to guard literary treasures. Everyone who knew him, including many visitors from Australia over the years, speaks glowingly of Feri's and Ilu's kindness, wit and intelligence. Then his sight began to fail. Vital tests were neglected and prominent doctors failed to give him the most basic attention and care in safeguarding his vision. This poor man became blind, bedridden and waiting for God. I am certain that he will have had a wonderful reception.

The Grosz Family

The surviving descendants of my mother's cousins who perished in 1944 now comprise my closest relatives. They – the Grosz family – live in Paris and I discovered them almost miraculously after being unaware of their existence for forty years.

My father's family was smaller and they lived in the country so I never knew them well. Most of the family I have known were on my mother's side. Gyula and Lili Grosz lived very close to our apartment in Buda. My small primary school was adjacent to their flat. It was on that street, just outside the building where the Grosz family lived, that I watched the Wehrmacht panzers roar into Budapest, crossing the Miklós Horthy Bridge over the Danube. That was the only bridge designed to support those tons of steel.

The Grosz parents looked after me while my mother took a rare holiday in the country, and I was in their home when the Allied invasion of North Africa in 1942 took place. I remember the headlines. The Grosz were charming, friendly, gregarious people. In 1944, they were taken by the Arrow Cross and murdered.

They had two children: János (known as Jancsi), and Éva, who both survived. Éva was a teacher, married to a professor of physiology; sadly she was struck down by polio during the global epidemic in the late forties. She had two children in spite of being confined to a wheelchair after her incomplete recovery from this dreadful illness. Her children became academics in teaching and music. Éva's husband Mátyás was a distinguished physiologist, totally loyal to his wife over the decades of her chronic and permanent disability. János escaped from Budapest towards the end of the war. He is the main link in this story of my relationship with the Grosz family.

Feri, Gyula's older brother, and his wife Mariska, were observant Jews. Feri was the head of a small Jewish community in Buda. He attended my Bar Mitzvah after the war, in sad circumstances, when six boys had a ceremony together, all of them having lost their fathers during the Holocaust. Mariska Grosz had Italian ancestry. She told me that in 1944 a distant relative was the commander of a partisan brigade in Italy who captured Mussolini. When I hear this story I start singing 'Bella Ciao', the song of the Italian partisans. Feri's daughter Ilonka had rheumatic fever as a child, and developed complications related to heart disease. She was married with a son, but became very disabled and died prematurely. Cardiac surgery was not sufficiently advanced in Hungary in the 1970s to offer her relief. She was a charming lady, a great loss to her family and all her friends.

János was a restless child, unsettled at school and at work. When he saw the climate of hate gathering in Hungary he saw little point in planning a long-term future. His sister Éva was quite different, being hard working and ambitious. János had many friends of whom his parents disapproved, because they had contempt for conventions, lacked ambition, and held left-wing political views.

Between 1949 and 1965 I lost all contact with all my relatives in Hungary. In 1981, however, I arranged for relatives from Budapest to meet me in Paris. We booked into my favourite hotel on the left bank, the Hotel des Balcons, where I had stayed during many visits over the decades. Situated close to the Theater Nationale-Odeon, it has a small statue at its entrance honouring the great poet Endre Ady, inscribed with his words: *'Paris est ecrit toujours dans mon coeur.'* This hotel had been Ady's favourite in the pre-war years. That year was my sabbatical from the university. It was a great joy to meet my relatives from Budapest. In addition they had got in touch with a lady in Paris, whose address they had obtained. I had to be dragged along to meet people whose existence I did not even suspect. It turned out that I was about to be reunited with a lost part of my family.

Marie-Claude, the widow of our cousin János Grosz who had died in Paris in the mid-1960s, was a schoolteacher working in the Ministry of Education, charming, bilingual and resourceful. Her own family came from the south-west of France, and amongst her family heirlooms she had medals and citations awarded to her forebears before the French Revolution. She was disowned by her family after the war for marrying my cousin, who was a Jew, a refugee and poor to boot. For the past thirty years, since soon after meeting János, and later after she became a widow (János died aged only forty-five in 1965), she had not heard from the rest of his family. This kindled a strong desire amongst their five children to discover the family roots on their father's side. János and Marie-Claude's children were brought up as a typical French family, and had virtually no knowledge of their father's background. Of his five children only the eldest knew his father as an adult. Marie-Claude managed, with a single salary, to bring up and educate five intelligent children. They are now working in a variety of fields, from banking to computers, teaching and running a restaurant.

Marie-Claude 'adopted' her late husband's remaining family in Hungary. She has kept in contact with them, trying to find out details of the family, as her husband had always been very reticent about his past and origins. He was scarred by his terrifying experiences in the Holocaust. At a dinner with the family in Paris the youngest son suddenly confronted me with the question: 'What about my father's Jewish origins?' Although it was painful to relate the story, I felt they needed to know. I asked Marie-Claude if I should speak. 'Yes, they must know', she replied, yielding to her son's request. I then told my cousins about János and his parents.

In the period of impending Nazi deportations to Auschwitz in 1944, János and Éva were hidden by their uncle in an orchard. After the fanatic Arrow Cross ran amok, all Jews were ordered on pain of death to report to a sports stadium. Many obeyed what to us seemed a death warrant. I recall discussing the official order to report for deportation with my mother at the time. Because of our recent near-fatal encounter with the Arrow Cross at the military barracks, we were never again going to be meekly led to slaughter and, fortunately, we refused to appear. Gyula Grosz and his wife Lili did however obey, and so were among the forty thousand victims of what became known as the 'Eichmann death march'.

From the sports stadium Jews were driven by gendarmes and Arrow Cross militia on foot to the Austrian border 120 kilometres away. They had to endure the cruelty of teenage service men in paramilitary uniform tormenting and brutalising them. Stragglers who fell, those who were frail or elderly, anyone who had any property the terrorists coveted (such as a good pair of leather boots), were mercilessly shot. Many hanged themselves on trees during overnight stops. Some died suffering exposure in the bitter frost. The corpses were left where they fell. The road from Budapest showed evidence of this carnage. The scene provoked adverse comments – even German Nazi generals were, according to numerous witnesses, less sadistic and merciless than the gendarmes and the Arrow Cross. Himmler, travelling on the road, ordered an immediate cessation of the death marches, but Eichmann resisted the order. Gyula and Lili Grosz escaped from the death marches and hid in a barn at Sopron near the border with Austria, but they were betrayed and shot. They are among the few members of my family whose mode of death is clearly known.

In the 1950s their son János was too close to this family tragedy to speak about it. He wanted his children to be simply French, human and unscarred. Of their father János I could add little more. He escaped in 1945 to join the French Foreign Legion, and was posted to Algeria and later Indochina. He

Frank Vajda, ca 1940

László Vajda, father, 1944

Mária Vajda, mother, 1949

Mother and Frank Vajda, Steyr, 1950

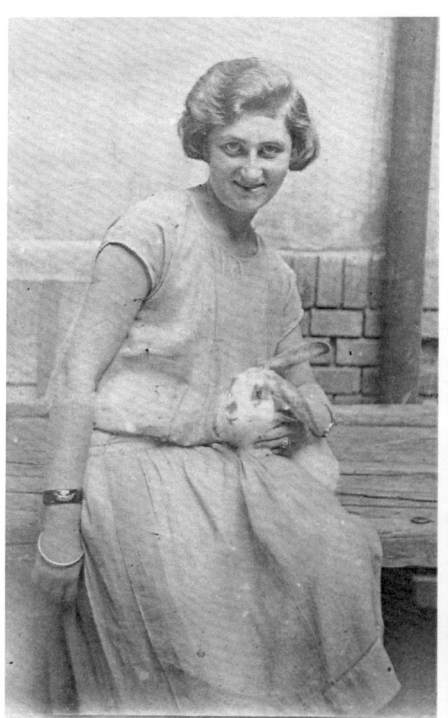

Mother, 1930 and 1951, on boat to Australia

Jonás Menedelssohn, great grandfather

Anna Weiss, maternal grandmother, and young Frank, 1938

Rózsa Mendelssohn, grandmother

Imre Keve, uncle, a chemical engineer, 1933

Mariska and Nándor Grosz, 1970   Father and Uncle Bandi, 1932

Feri and Ilu Falus, Paris, 1981   Mother and Bandi, rowing on the Danube, 1932

Anna Keve, grandmother

Dr Albert Molnár, uncle, a lawyer, Budapest, 1950

Rózsa Vajda, grandmother, and young Frank   Father, Bandi and Zsigmond Vajda, grandfather

Aniko and András Waldapfel (front centre and back right, respectively), cousins (died Auschwitz, 1944)

Back: Steven (died Ukraine, c. 1942), Nàndor (died c. 1941) and Feri
Front: Uncle John, Margit (shot in Danube, Arrow Cross, 2 January 1945), Nellie and Mother

New Year's Eve, 1938, Father (on extreme left in second row, with glasses) and G. Waldapfel (to left and above)

Back: Children and K. Molnar (centre), M. Gerbner and A. Molnar
Front: H. Graber and I. Boc with children

Alice Weiss Hospital

Regent Miklós Horthy

Albrecht Barracks, 1970

International Refugee Organization
International Tracing Service
Headquarters
APO 171 US. Army

Organisation Internationale pour les Réfugiés
Service International de Recherches
Siège Central

Certificate of Incarceration
Certificat d'Incarcération
Bescheinigung über Inhaftierung

№ 11314/CI-9061

1. Reference your enquiry for certificate of incarceration for:
   Faisant suite à votre demande de certificat d'incarcération pour:

   Name / Nom: **VAJDA**
   First names / Prénoms: **Ladislaus**
   Nationality / Nationalité: **Hungarian**

   Date of birth / Date de naissance: **14 April 1907**
   Place of birth / Lieu de naissance: **Marosvasarhely**
   Prisoner's No. / No. de Prisonnier: **119397**

2. It is hereby certified that the following information is available in documentary evidence held by the International Tracing Service.
   Il est certifié par la présente que les informations suivantes se trouvent dans la documentation détenue par le Service International de Recherches.
   Es wird hiermit bestätigt, daß folgende Angaben in der Dokumentation des Internationalen Suchdienst aufgeführt sind.

   Name / Nom: **VAJDA**
   First names / Prénoms: **Ladislaus**

   Date of birth: **14 April 1907**
   Place of birth: **Marovasakerly**
   Nationality: **Hungarian**

   Last permanent residence / Dernière adresse connue: **not given**

   ~~Has entered~~ concentration camp / est entré au camp de concentration: **Mauthausen**
   Prisoner's No. / No. de prisonnier: **119397**

   on / le: **25 January 1945**
   coming from / venant de: **Auschwitz Concentration Camp**

   Reason given for incarceration / Raison donnée pour l'incarcération: **"Jude"**

   ~~Executrix~~ He died on 7 March 1945 at 1035 hours in Con. Camp Ebensee (Kommando ~~Fronium~~ of Mauthausen) - Cause of Death: "akute Herzschwaeche".

   Liberated/Released on / Libéré/Relâché le: _____ in / à _____

   Remarks / Remarques: **none**

3. References of documents / Références des documents: **"Nummernbuecher (OCC 15/145 + 15/1) Totenbuch 1945 Nr. 5762, Veraenderungsmeldungen"** of the Mauthausen Concentration Camp documents. -

   Arolsen, 6th July 1950

   Signature
   Rene EVERAERT
   Deputy Director of the International Tracing Service
   Directeur Adjoint du Service International de Recherches

Certificate from Mauthausen Incarceration: "Jude"

Marktgemeinde Mauthausen
Standesamt
Zl.: 190/530/50

Mauthausen, am 20. April 1950

Bescheinigung.

Das Standesamt Mauthausen bescheinigt hiemit, daß in den hier aufliegenden Listen des ehemaligen KZ Lagers Mauthausen der Ungarische Jude Vajda Ladislaus, geboren am 14. April 1907 unter der Häftlingsnummer 119 397 eingetragen ist und sein Sterbedatum der 7. März 1945 in der Liste verzeichnet ist.

Der Standesbeamte:
/ Blaha /

Death Certifcate from Mauthausen Incarceration: 7 March 1945, "Heart Failure"

Concentration camp, Ebensee (KZ Mauthausen)

Ebensee Memorial Tower

Memorial of the Hungarian Jewish Martyrs, Dohány Street Synagogue, inscribed with names of victims

Ebensee Memorial Arch

Memorial to Murdered Victims of Nazism. Removed by Austrians as "inconvenient" about 25 years later

Individual memorial

Mass graves, Ebensee

Raoul Wallenberg Street, Budapest, 1947

Butchers of Hungarian Jewry, László Endre and László Baky, being executed

Farago Dezső and Sándor Barta, slave labourers, died 1945

Ervin Révai, whose mother was deported from a funeral in 1944

Imre Trencsényi Waldapfel, Mother's cousin, Chancellor of the University of Budapest

Dr Leslie Balázs, close friend, whose brother was a messenger of Wallenberg, shot by Arrow Cross

Frank Vajda in 2008 with a soldier of the Russian Army involved in liberating Budapest from Nazis in 1945

Dr Peter Barta, son of Sándor Barta, with Peter Handelsman, son of deported Géza Handelsman, and his wife Anne

SVÉD VÖRÖSKERESZT
MAGYARORSZÁGI KIRENDELTSÉGÉNEK
TUDÓSÍTÓ OSZTÁLYA
BUDAPEST, 82.

Budapest, 194 4 nov. 8

V É D L E V É L.

Ezennel hivatalosan igazoljuk, hogy Simkovits Sándorné a SVÉD KIRÁLYI KÖVETSÉG mellett működő SVÉD VÖRÖSKERESZT magyarországi kirendeltsége oltalomlevelének birtokában van. Kérjük a Hatóságokat, hogy a H.M.I52.730./ELN.42/44.sz. rendelet értelmében ezt a körülményt a legteljesebb mértékben vegyék tekintetbe és ennek értelmében járjanak el.

Név: Simkovics Sándorné sz. László Erzsébet
Szül.: Perkáta I9o9 jul.5
Anyja neve: Kellner Irma
Haja: Szőke
Szeme: Kék
Mag.: I6o

Főmegbizott.

Swedish Red Cross protection paper, 1944

Boston University

ELIE WIESEL
University Professor and
Andrew W. Mellon Professor in the Humanities

745 Commonwealth Avenue
Boston, Massachusetts 02215
617/353-4566

January 16, 2002

Professor Frank Vajda, Director
Australian Centre for Clinical Neuropharmacology
Raoul Wallenberg Centre
41 Victoria Pde;
Fitzroy Vic., 3065, Australia

Dear Professor Vajda:

    Thanks for your recent letter. I am pleased to accept your invitation to join the Honorary Board of your Raoul Wallenberg Centre. The work you are doing is important and of course, what Raoul Wallenberg represents is well-known to me, and therefore, I am happy to have my name associated with the Centre that bears his name.

    With best wishes,

Elie Wiesel

EW/mlh

tried to escape repeatedly, once by trying to swim across the Suez Canal, but he was caught. Finally, he was allowed to leave the Legion in the 1950s. Éva, János's sister, also died prematurely, ten years after him.

The present Grosz family, whose grandparents were murdered by Hitler, now, decades later, comprise nine grandchildren, and at least ten great-grandchildren, all descendants of Gyula and Lili. Two of the grandchildren live in Budapest, the city of their grandparents. Five of them who live in France are coming to terms with their background. Lili and Gyula would have been proud of them.

The Waldapfel Family

One of the most loved and fondly remembered branches of the family were the Waldapfels, who were my grandmother's first cousins. János Waldapfel was a pedagogue who became headmaster of one of the elite schools in Budapest, the Trefort-utca Gymnasium, or University Training High School (Minta Gimnazium). This gymnasium nurtured the talents of many internationally known mathematicians, physicists and economists, including Hans von Neumann, founder of modern computer theory, Lord Balogh and Lord Kaldor, economic overlords in Britain under Harold Wilson in the 1960s, and Leo Szilard and Edward Teller, 'fathers' of the atom bomb and the hydrogen bomb respectively. It was largely János Waldapfel's name and prestige, many years after his death, which helped me to get admitted into that school after the war.

The Waldapfels had five children, each of whom were prominent figures in their fields, though tragically only three survived after 1944. Gábor, the eldest, became managing director of the Weiss Manfréd subsidiary, Globus Foods. Weiss Manfréd was a major industrial conglomerate in the heavy industry sector in Hungary. It produced aeroplanes, cars, motorcycles, weapons and other items, so it became a prime target for acquisition by the Nazis. Goering and the SS competed for it, and being a Jewish-owned firm, it was defenceless. It was acquired by the Goering Works, and the Waldapfel family of thirty-two members were allowed to flee to Portugal after receiving a nominal compensation for handing over the firm. Globus was the trademark of the prominent food processing division. The company continued to exist, even after the post-war Communist takeover; it produces of some of the tastiest canned food products in Europe.

Gábor helped my father get a job in Globus, where he had worked until dismissed by the restrictions imposed on Jews. Gábor was obviously a very able man, and featured on the Germans' arrest list of prominent Jews from the first day of occupation; he was soon taken, in March 1944. A signed postcard arrived from 'Waldsee' – this was a cynical cover-up of the actual destination of deportees, who were sent to the Auschwitz gas chambers soon after the card was sent. Gábor's wife Erzsébet and their children, András, who was my age, and Anikó, aged thirteen, were deported together to Auschwitz two months later, when the outer suburbs of Budapest, including Pestszenterzsebet, were emptied of their Jewish population. They never returned. András was under ten years of age, and so did not have a chance; not being *arbeitsfähig* (capable of work), he was murdered on arrival. Anikó being older, strong and brave, apparently answered back to a Kapo or an SS overseer and was promptly despatched to the gas chambers as punishment, although physically she was robust and initially selected for slave labour.

Esther Waldapfel, a sister of Gábor and daughter of János and his wife, was an ebullient, large, dark haired lady. After Liberation in 1945 she became Director of the Hungarian State Archives, a position of considerable prestige. She survived partly by luck, as most of those who survived can testify they did also, and partly aided by her marriage to an Aryan husband. She left no children.

Her brother Imre Trencsényi Waldapfel was the closest to my immediate family. Born on the same day as my mother, he was a pure 'ivory tower' intellectual, an academic and a prolific author of original as well as interpretive articles of literature. He wrote and translated tracts from six languages but could not hold a conversation using any of them. He was a noted expert on Greek mythology and published several volumes on this formidable subject. He was made Professor in the largest provincial city of Hungary, at Szeged, before returning to the capital to become Head of Classical Studies at the university in Budapest, and a member of the Hungarian National Academy. Later he was appointed Chancellor of the University of Budapest.

Many decades later, on a visit to Budapest, I was speaking to my cousin Hedwig Graber, later to become an acclaimed Professor of Clinical Pharmacology. We met my cousin Imre-András, son of the classical scholar, Imre Waldapfel. The two had never met previously. Hedwig exclaimed: 'Is it not a strange coincidence that we meet now, when fifty years ago your father, Imre, as Chancellor of the University, handed me my medical degree.' My mother respected Imre Snr very highly, but at the time of our escape from Hungary, she did not confide in him. She knew he had firm views about the rosy future of Communism and she distrusted his judgment. How wise she was, in this instance as well as in many others. Imre junior, my cousin, sixty years later admitted as much: 'If only my parents had the insight to leave this country, we would have been so much better and happier in every way.'

Imre Snr adopted the Hungarian surname Trencsényi and coupled it to his original name as Trencsényi-Waldapfel. He did so, I believe, to distinguish himself from his equally prominent brother József, who was slightly senior to him. It was Imre Snr who edited the posthumous poems of the major figure in Hungarian literature, Miklós Radnóti, who was executed by his Nazi Hungarian guards in 1945 when he was terminally weak and no hospital would accept a Jewish slave labourer for treatment. The poet's notebook was found in his clothes in the mass grave at Abda in Hungary where he was buried. Imre, who is remembered widely and with great affection, left three children, all of whom follow the family tradition of education, languages and social sciences.

The third Waldapfel son was József, but quite unlike Joseph Stalin, my uncle Joe was no dictator. He was nonetheless a powerful personality at the peak of his career as Secretary for the Ministry of Culture, Professor of Hungarian Language and Literature at the National University of Budapest, Cultural Ambassador for the People's Republic, and a strong influence in education. He was influential in shaping post-war Communist theory as applied to the development of Hungary, a Soviet satellite. In his earlier life uncle Joe had studied for a number of years in a yeshiva, a Jewish rabbinical college, and later became a teacher, and then a university lecturer. His meteoric rise after Liberation was partly due to his embracing the new idol of Communism after the old one of orthodox Judaism. It is said, however, that thirty years later he reverted to Judaism as the dominant dogma in his life. He had married ten years before the outbreak of World War Two, and had one daughter, who was somewhat eccentric even as a child. She had fantasies of becoming an actress or an entertainer, and was enrolled in a ballet school, aged six, to learn the fundamentals of dancing. I still recall with considerable embarrassment a birthday party, where cousins had to endure little Annuska, as she was called, demonstrating her newly acquired ballet skills and being asked, as a small boy, to see if I could emulate her. It was an acutely painful moment, as I had never seen anything like this before. I had to pirouette and do simple ballet manoeuvres in front of amused relatives, and was laughed at. Uncle Joe and his family survived the Holocaust, but after the war we saw little of them, due to the turbulence of events and the total disarrangement of our lives.

When we left Hungary, in August 1949, I recall somewhat dramatically spitting on its soil with contempt as we waded across the frontier at the Ipoly River. Migrating to Australia was a most wonderful choice, which I owe totally, and profoundly gratefully, to my dear Mother. Twenty-five years later I went back to visit Budapest for the sake of relatives. Somehow I got in touch with uncle Joe. He was keen to invite me, with other relatives from different branches of the family, for a big reunion dinner. It was partly to welcome me, and more importantly to announce that Annuska was getting married and her bridegroom was to be introduced. The poignant thing, which affected me most, was that uncle Joe picked a famous restaurant next to Parliament as the site of the reunion. It was this same restaurant, called Elysee, where thirty years earlier my father took me for a memorable lunch, one year before the destruction of our lives. He was unemployed and impoverished, but he felt he should take me to a wonderful restaurant at least once, for who knows what comes next. It was a prophetic gesture. I saw him only a few times after that meal. The lunch we had at the Elysee will be forever etched in my memory, and I am still overcome seventy-five years later when I think of that occasion.

Uncle Joe had hired this restaurant. About forty members of the family, some of whom I have never known, were invited. Annuska was there, about six months pregnant. Before leaving Budapest three days later I rang uncle Joe to thank him for the dinner. He said he was sorry he could not see me to say goodbye. Three hours later I was waiting in the departure lounge at Ferihegy airport. Suddenly an enormous, black, chauffeur driven limousine pulled up outside the building. A strong, corpulent man jumped out, came up to me, kissed me, put his arms around me, and then left without a word. It was my uncle Joseph. I never saw him again, as he passed away soon after.

The Pudler Family

In 1965, when I returned for a visit to Hungary for the first time in fifteen years, it was because, in spite of me having no desire to return, I had been told by a family friend, who had always spoken warmly of my relatives, 'I think one of your uncles is still alive in Russia. I remember hearing about him on the radio many years ago. A.V., an architect, is working in the USSR where he has been decorated for building a sports stadium for the Soviet Union'. She urged me to put in a request to the Red Cross to see if they could find out details about his captivity, or his circumstances.

I agreed and contacted the Red Cross who accepted the request. I had almost forgotten about the enquiry, when two years later a letter arrived, an answer from the Red Cross Searching Service, a most impressive document. The letter stated that they had been unable to find my uncle, who, it was believed, had died in Soviet captivity. However they had located a long lost relative, Elizabeth Pudler, who was my father's cousin. She was a legal counsellor to the national daily newspaper in Budapest and a member of the memorial committee of Holocaust survivors. She had been through the Auschwitz nightmare, survived it and returned to live in Hungary. Elizabeth had asked the Red Cross for my address, and wished to resume contact, which had been lost since 1945. After considerable soul searching I gave her my address. I remembered her well, but memories of her were less than agreeable.

A few weeks later a letter arrived, which was so ingratiating it made me cringe. She addressed the letter to both my mother and myself, inviting us both to visit her in Budapest. She wrote that she thought of us a great deal, and regretted the incident that caused us to sever all contact. She wanted to resume friendship with us, as her only surviving relative, her ninety-five year old mother, was suffering from dementia. Elizabeth did not know that my mother had died seven years previously, and that I had not forgotten the suffering she had caused many years earlier.

It was a story of greed, aggression and stupidity. My mother helped my grandmother, her mother-in-law, to survive the war, the siege, the Holocaust and starvation, by hiding her with us in the safe house where she had worked. After Liberation my grandmother returned to the family apartment. Her two beautiful sons, my father and uncle, did not return. She was miserable and died four months after Liberation, possibly by taking her own life. Mother arranged the funeral, cleaned up the flat, and then had to wind up the apartment. She advertised to sell the contents. At that point, some weeks after the funeral, cousin Elizabeth arrived. One afternoon I went to help Mother clean up grandmother's flat. I found my mother being rudely shouted at by this harridan of a woman, ten years her junior. She called my mother a hyena, accused her of robbing the dead, and claimed the property as her own, as she was a relative, my grandmother's niece. Preposterous behaviour, given the fact that I was alive and it was my grandmother's property and Elizabeth's role had been negligible, even non-existent.

My mother was devastated and ashen-faced. She tried to explain her plight over these months, the hard choices and lack of support, without any sign of assistance from Elizabeth's side of the family. It was of no use as Elizabeth was hysterical. As so often in the past – and I am very happy to relate this – my mother turned to me and asked: 'What shall we do with her?' I remember the phrasing: 'What can we do with this woman?' I was absolutely sick with anxiety and concern for Mother, and felt humiliated and under siege, so I replied: 'We shall leave, and never talk to her again. We shall leave it all to her, if that is what she wants.' This is what happened, and we never heard any trace of her again, until her letter arrived twenty years later. The fact that in her letter she had invited my mother made me feel better. I wrote and explained that my mother had died. By return mail another letter arrived, even more loving, saying she wanted to adopt me – I was thirty years old at the time – as her only surviving relative.

On my next trip to Europe I looked her up in Budapest, aware that she was very fragile emotionally. She was much older than me, obviously very clever, but manipulative and depressed. Her mother was in her last phase of life, barely able to communicate. Elizabeth wanted me to have presents, which I declined; in particular I refused to visit her office to 'show me off', as she worked in the offices of the Communist Party newspaper. She could not understand the reason. She gave me the last photograph taken of my father, and a nail file which he gave Elizabeth on his last visit, at the funeral of my grandfather. I reflected that, though it was not meant to be, this small instrument may have been sufficient for him to cut through the floor of the cattle truck carrying him to the death camp.

Later, strolling in the city, she took me to a bookshop. I wanted nothing, but in the end I bought Simon Wiesenthal's book, *The Murderers Amongst Us*, which, as I found out later from Wiesenthal in person, was the earliest of his books published in the Eastern bloc, printed in Romania. Simon Wiesenthal devoted his life to tracking down former Nazis, and for this he became a hero of mine. Elizabeth was mortally offended when I could not visit her mother on my two day visit to Budapest. In spite of her recent kindness, I had not forgiven her for the attack on my mother and lost touch with her after the second visit.

Chapter Seven

THE FATE OF OTHERS

Hunger

I was once asked on Vatican Radio, which is an instrument of reconciliation and peace, to comment on forgetting and forgiving the crimes of the Holocaust. I said that it is not up to me to forgive. I am not fit to offer forgiveness for crimes committed against others. For the crimes against me I cannot forgive, even though I know that is not orthodox teaching. Regarding forgetting, how can I forget that my father died of starvation? I cannot leave a spoonful of food on my plate, without thinking that my father could have been saved if he had been offered that spoonful. This opinion came to be broadcast in Hungary and displayed on the websites of many Catholic and Protestant churches in Hungary and neighbouring countries.

Because of my father's fate of starving to death after nine months of incarceration in various camps, I never leave any food on a plate after a meal. Whatever I am offered, or what I have, I eat. I never throw away food. To me hunger has deep meaning for nothing compares to dying of starvation. I am still appalled at the waste we tolerate in the West, especially at social functions, where a sizable portion of the food is thrown out. I am amazed at regulations which prevent it being given to the needy, and I have nothing but contempt for people who routinely leave half their portion of food on their plate, as though it were the most natural thing to do. They obviously have not had my experience, nor the experience of millions who starve each day.

After the siege of Budapest, the whole population was starving. I recall an incident when my mother and relatives found a pot of beans in a kitchen. They threw themselves at it and devoured it ravenously from the same pot, cold and not totally fresh, but not before asking me if I wanted some. I declined – the reason was that I had never starved. My mother in the critical weeks of the siege of Budapest managed to cook a chicken and kept it frozen, stored in a jar in chicken fat and carefully rationed to me each day. She never tasted it. One morning she was crying with anger and frustration. A dog, which must have also been starving, had found the jar and ate my precious chicken leg. There was nothing to be done, but seeing my family devouring that bean stew made me realise the depth of hunger everybody felt at that time. There was no meat to be had.

As a young man, on Yom Kippur I used to fast. In 1965 the Day of Atonement coincided with the most important day for my postgraduate medical examination in Edinburgh. The examination went from early morning till the early afternoon, and hunger does not sit well with extreme concentration and attempts at higher achievement. I had a choice: shall I have a delicious Scottish breakfast of bacon and eggs, tea, toast, marmalade and fruit? Or fast and predictably get a horrible migraine and fail the examination? I chose the pragmatic way out: I ate and passed. A colleague some time later said that God would not give a fig whether I had bacon and eggs for breakfast or not.

Tamás Dub

In a letter to a friend in 2014 I wrote, among other things: 'In connection with your former father-in-law, nicknamed "Sruel" [Israel], I thank you for telling me what this nickname signifies. I must explain to you why I can never use this as a nickname ever again.' In 1942–43 I had a classmate in the first two years of primary school, called Tamás Dub. We had attended a Jewish school, because elsewhere we would have been humiliated and jeered at. Tamás was the same age as me, good looking, amiable, with an ebullient personality. We both had a 'crush' on the same eight-year-old girl, but I was too shy or lacking in self-confidence ever to admit this to anyone. Thus Tom became the boyfriend of Kati Kis. Tamás, who had a Transylvanian background, lived with his parents in an apartment block close to us in Budapest.

At the end of 1943, when anti-Semitism was already rampant and the waves of hatred were threatening us, a Jewish Holy Day, Simchat Tora, was observed. It was an occasion when all those who could, and who were observant, built a hut in their garden and stayed there for a few nights. This was the Festival of Tabernacles. At the service in the temple, many of the children had a flag, nicely coloured with the Star of David and with Hebrew writing on it, flying on a small stick which they could wave around. After a class or after a service on the Sabbath morning, my friend Tamás ran out of the temple, waving his flag and singing Jewish songs, hurtling along Bocskay Road, in Lágymányos, a modest suburb of Budapest. I could not comprehend this, and was quite taken aback, as this boy did not realise at all what danger was threatening the Jewish people, and he was now showing off. At eight years of age he should have been warned. Tamás Dub and his parents left Budapest soon after, and returned to Transylvania, most probably believing that they would be liberated earlier than in Budapest, as the Russian armies were approaching from the east.

Unfortunately the first district from which Jews were deported, after the German occupation of Hungary, was Transylvania. So the first good friend I ever had, at the age of eight, ended his life in a gas chamber. The German bastards murdered him and his family. I visited him at his home on only one occasion. According to the custom in Budapest, the names of tenants in the various apartments were displayed on the front door. There it was: the name of Tamás Dub's father, Israel Dub. This is why I cannot use the nickname 'Sruel' in the future. Ever. For reasons of reverence and respect.

Table Football

As a child and adolescent I used to play a form of table football based on soccer. I have continued to indulge in this form of game for the past six decades, now even as an old man. The idea is to use buttons to represent soccer players. The contestants move their buttons alternately, aiming to hit a small button which represents a soccer ball, trying to get it into a miniature goal fashioned after the real thing. There are strict rules about foul play, penalties, corner kicks, and bringing the ball back into play. The game is widely played in central Europe, and has even achieved international status in competitions.

Of the six people participating in our annual competition played over a monthly series of matches, five are of Jewish origin, all from Hungary, all of them Holocaust survivors. The circumstances of their fathers' fate illustrate the divergence of fortunes that befell people during this period. Four of my friends lost their fathers in the Holocaust. They all have a poignant and remarkable story.

Bor

The first friend is an exception, as he is not actually a player of button soccer. Nevertheless, in spite of this failure in character, he is a thoroughly decent chap. He has never played any form of sport and would not know a cricket ball from a golf ball. He is also older than us, by an eternity of about four years. This is a significant time in the life of a child, as by virtue of his age he remembers early events in his childhood years which for me escape conscious recollection. This friend has a story about this father, different to those that follow.

Peter is the son of a mixed marriage – a so-called *Mischling*. As such, Nazi racial laws did apply to him, but the definition was always somewhat blurred, and depended, in addition to the number of Aryan grandparents one had, on your education and religious beliefs as a child. Peter's father was Jewish and was therefore subject to the ignoble slave labour legislation. Peter himself was sheltered by his mother and by virtue of his upbringing and appearance he evaded being persecuted. His father, Dezsõ Faragó, was a prominent writer and a charming intellectual.

As a result of the agreement between the Germans and the Horthy government, about 6000 Jewish servicemen were taken to the copper mines of Bor in Serbia. Their story is now part of the fabric of history, especially as one of their fellow slaves was the poet Miklós Radnóti. Radnóti's notebook, mentioned earlier, containing his work written in captivity, was found, damp and discoloured but legible, in the mass grave where he was buried after being shot by Hungarian escort guards. The notebook bore the inscription: 'Would the finder please return this book to Mr Ortutay', a writer who subsequently became a Minister of Cultural Affairs. Facsimile editions of Radnóti's notebook on Bor were published after Liberation.

At Bor, Peter's father suffered the indignities and maltreatment meted out to all slave labourers. When the time came to withdraw the contingent from Serbia because of the deteriorating military situation, Eichmann, the plenipotentiary for the 'Jewish question' in Hungary, was asked (as I later learnt) what was to happen to the prisoners. The Eichmann trial transcripts show that he issued a brief order: 'Retreat half and shoot the other half'. The surviving labourers were withdrawn in two columns on consecutive days. The first column passed through Serbian territory and the labourers were aided wherever possible by the kindness of the Serbian peasant population. When they reached Hungarian territory they were cursed and jeered. When the column arrived they expected to be released, but just then the Arrow Cross seized power in Budapest. The second column made an overnight stop in a village. The escorting SS systematically murdered them all by shooting them in batches. Peter's father was in the second contingent and perished. The first group did not fare much better, as after the Arrow Cross takeover, they were also attacked and many were killed. It is clear that the laws, which defined Jews racially and allowed some exemptions, were only of theoretical consideration. Once a victim was in their grasp, the Germans and their satellites treated them all with indiscriminate brutality.

The Cemetery (June 1944)

On the last day of June 1944 Mrs Elza Révai attended the funeral of her brother-in-law in Budapest. Arriving with the rest of her family, they were arrested and taken away by the gendarmes. The date 30 June 1944 marks the day when – allegedly – Horthy promised Per Anger, the Swedish envoy, that he would stop the deportations. In fact the last train left Budapest over a week later, at Eichmann's insistence. It is possible Elza Révai did not even reach Auschwitz. In spite of intensive searches, placing notices all over Budapest, her desperate family failed to locate her. Neighbours tried to find her name on death lists recently made available to Yad Vashem, but were unsuccessful. We shall probably never know her fate. Maybe the neighbours and relatives tried to spare each other's feelings. Ervin lost three aunts and an uncle, but his father fortunately returned from slave labour in Bor, Yugoslavia. Ervin Révai became a famous engineer associated with the design of the Stockholm indoor hockey stadium and remains the greatest button soccer player I have encountered in sixty years.

A Postcard

My poor friend Gaby's father, Jenő Schön, had a sad end. Gaby himself died recently after a long battle with heart disease. Just before he died he asked to be relieved of his misery; I could not help him, but his doctors were kind to him. The story he told me fifteen years ago is attested to by a postcard that I still have in my collection. On 19 March 1944 the Germans occupied Hungary. The Wehrmacht was accompanied by Eichmann's staff, the so-called *Sondereinsatz Kommando*, with its task to solve the 'Jewish question' in Hungary.

The task began immediately. Working from a prepared list obtained from telephone books, the Gestapo arrested and locked up several hundred prominent Jewish men and took them to Auschwitz as a 'test run'. Their numbers were swelled by those caught at railway stations, at funerals or by raids in the streets. Those unfortunate enough to be caught were deported. On arrival at Auschwitz, as touched on earlier, they had to sign a pre-printed postcard, which informed their families that they were well looked after, were working in good conditions, had adequate food and housing, and were looking forward to re-uniting with their families soon. The postcard had a sender's address imprinted on it: Waldsee. After sending the postcard they were gassed and cremated. The relatives were deceived and overjoyed, and pored over the maps to locate Waldsee. It was not on the map, a fictitious address. But it achieved its purpose to some degree – it calmed the relatives and prevented panic, strengthening the hands of those who urged caution, rational behaviour and collaboration, the official *Judenrat* (Jewish Council) policy. The end result: people from the provinces, deported largely to Auschwitz in just over six weeks, perished. Jenő Schön, as his family found out after Liberation, was transferred to another camp at Muhldorf and died at the end of 1944 of heart failure, a term in German doublespeak meaning murdered by starvation.

The Knock on the Door

Peter is a writer steeped in his native tongue, but to make a living he was forced to become a businessman. He left Hungary in similar circumstances to Gaby. They had been friends for decades before they joined our soccer group. His story is very brief. In October 1944 the Hungarian extreme right Arrow Cross took over the reigns of government. Any facade of legitimacy was dropped, and it became a battle for extermination or survival. People became desperately afraid; Jews were murdered on the spot, shot in the river or in Party houses, or made to go on death marches. Peter, aged nine, was hiding in a flat, which was officially sealed as a sign of it being abandoned. He was sheltered under total silence from the rampaging mobs. A knock on the door, then a more insistent knock. The inhabitants cower in terror. A voice: 'Please open. I am Géza, your father. Open the door. Please!' The inhabitants confer. The decision is to maintain silence for their collective safety. The knocking weakens, the father is turned away. The knocking stops. He is never seen again. Later enquiries reveal that the Bad Arolsen Nazi archives made available to Yad Vashem contained a Gestapo entry that Ervin Handelsmann's life was ended at Buchenwald. It is documented with grotesquely misplaced German precision confirming the day, hour and minute of his passing. David's wife is an artist. Her grandmother, Josephine Berta Kohn is seen in the famous 'Auschwitz album' – a book of photographs taken by professional SS cameramen and published after the war – walking slowly on the road to the Auschwitz gas chambers.

A Cigarette

The fifth friend, Peter, also became an orphan in 1944. I do not know the exact circumstances, but his father was in a slave labour camp, at Turkheim in the closing stages of the war. The Germans felt compelled to continue their torture and mass murder of Jews, particularly those held captive in the camps. With no apparent purpose other than inhumanity and hatred, they moved, marched, shunted, starved and worked to death the majority of survivors of the camps, intermittently speeding up the process with full scale massacres. Many thousands died of deprivation. Food, water, sanitation, clothing, medicines were non-existent, only beatings and executions were plentiful. My friend's father was a heavy smoker. Even more than the lack of food, he suffered from the withdrawal of smoking. He was starved like all others, but he made starvation even more lethal, hastening his end by exchanging his food rations for cigarettes. He could not be saved. Perhaps Sándor Barta did not wish to live any longer.

Chapter Eight

POST-WAR HUNGARY

Kindergarten

My schooling started during the later years of the Holocaust, and I had only eighteen months at school before our lives were shattered. My immersion in the world of knowledge started at the age of five at a kindergarten, which was situated about ten minutes' walk from our home. It was in an old house amidst a nice garden on top of a hill just above the 'Bottomless Lake' in Buda, one of the lesser known landmarks of the capital. It was an unusual kindergarten, in that the language of the teaching, or rather the tenor of the place, was German, not the dominant language of Hungary. German was spoken largely by the educated classes: the ethnic Germans and the Jewish people. The two matrons who ran the place were refugees from Hitler. What better way to earn a living than to teach children the joys of a language associated with their homeland, and at the same time also related to their plight.

The reason I was sent there, I suspect, was my parents' desire, and especially my grandmother's, to make me linguistically proficient at an early age, as part of a general education, and partly because my family spoke German well. We could not afford a nanny, so kindergarten had to suffice. My native tongue was Hungarian – I spoke no other language until I was nine years of age, when I started learning English. The attempt to make me speak German was a dismal failure. Like every other child in the class, I learnt nothing, except to ask the teacher to go to the toilet, and to specify the nature of the need. The only other phrase I learnt specially, not at kindergarten, but at home, was a phrase that parents used when not wanting the child to understand: *Nicht vor dem Kind*, meaning 'not in front of the child'. Or they would change languages.

One of the children attending my kindergarten was the niece of Miklós Kállay, Prime Minister of Hungary, who in the face of overwhelming pressures courageously tried to prevent the occupation of Hungary for two years, and refused to surrender the Jews to Hitler. Another memory from my initial exposure to a wider society at the kindergarten was that some children habitually used foul language, especially when it came to abusing other children, using the appellation 'filthy Jew'. I did not quite know what that meant, but it was soon explained, and so I was introduced to anti-Semitism. Partly in response to this and partly due to the fact that Jewish children were likely to be beaten up or molested at state schools, my parents enrolled me in the local Jewish school, the only such school I ever attended, and that only for eighteen months. The year was 1942, the year of Stalingrad and North Africa. Things looked grim. My father was away at slave labour, as indeed were all the male members of the family, including my beloved uncle.

Primary Education

The school I attended was small and friendly, called the Baracs Karoly Izraelita Elemi. I remember being apprehensive, as I could not write well, and could read only slowly. I feared I would be expected to know everything straight away. I wonder if that is a normal reaction for school children? Do they fear that their ignorance is going to be exposed?

The teacher was a kind and friendly lady, Teri Barta, wife of the headmaster, also an active teacher. I did well, but the prizes went to other children, who were refugees from Nazism, often from broken families and not even speaking the language well. The ethos of the school was that they were in greater need of support, and the prizes carried a modest amount of money. I am glad in retrospect we were able to help those families, who probably suffered more in the conflagration which followed.

The Bartas had two children, both at the same school. The whole family was killed by the Arrow Cross, who dumped them in the Danube in October of that fateful year. In 1942 a handful of Slovakian refugee children, who were totally dispossessed, joined us. We were told not to ask any questions. They were housed, fed and clothed by the local community, and they remained at the school until the German occupation. Then they suddenly disappeared. Only many years later did I learn that it was likely they fell victim to an infamous decision by the Hungarian Government which resulted in the massacre of twenty thousand people who could not prove their continuous residence in the country for the past forty years.

My second year at primary school started in late 1943, but lasted only six months, from September till March 1944. Those years carry sad connotations.

On March 19 the Wehrmacht arrived. My little school was fifty metres away from the road leading to that only bridge capable of bearing the weight of the Panzer tanks. They all rolled in, massive frightening columns, with airplanes flying overhead. The populace welcomed them. School was closed as the occupiers designated it as a stable for the amazing number of horses they had. The only other time I saw the school was after the occupation; it was filthy, neglected, a complete mess, and the mountains of horse manure reminded me, quite fittingly, of the SS.

Teaching re-opened, however, in an atmosphere of acute apprehension, at a local synagogue, where the same teachers battled against increasingly difficult conditions to maintain a semblance of normality and hope. Laws restricting Jewish life in all facets – travel, employment, dwellings, finance, communication, confiscations – rolled on relentlessly. The yellow star to be worn on clothes was made compulsory for everyone above the age of six. As part of my education, I recall being laughed at by the son of a concierge of a housing estate for wearing the yellow star. But I also remember with gratitude a circuit judge, a man with an aristocratic name, and I honour him by recalling it, Dr József Mátéffy, who lived in our building, witnessed my torment, and told the evil little bastard who was taunting me that 'he ought to be ashamed of himself". There were few like him. My former friends from the playground vanished when I appeared with the yellow star. It was unbelievably painful to walk on the street even for a few hours after this and to be exposed to mockery.

Fortunately schools closed soon after, as the provincial deportations of the Jews were about to begin. We were evicted from our flat by an order from the Housing Ministry and were, as noted earlier, fortunate to be taken in by Mother's employers, the hospital where she had trained. It was a midwifery institute and eventually came to house three hundred frightened refugees awaiting the Final Solution. My education continued even in this ghetto, which was the closest equivalent to a 'protected' house. One middle-aged lady, Margit Néni, happened to be one of the inmates of the hospital. One day in October, some months since I had received any formal teaching, it was agreed that she would try to teach children in the crowded, difficult conditions. I had a number of lessons in the basement hall, which was the ante-room to the emergency department. After a while we settled into a routine. Some weeks later we were attacked at night by Nazi terrorists, who made people crowd into our class room, threatening immediate execution. Eventually they were prevailed upon to make a selection of Jewish people on the basis of their protective documents. After hours of terror under the barrels of guns, thirty-five people were selected for further processing. As we found out a few days later, they were shot and thrown into the river. My poor teacher Margit was one of those taken, together with my relatives.

School After Liberation

Following Liberation by the Red Army in 1945, I had to think about resuming schooling. Since starting in 1943 I had only had eighteen months of primary education, and I was by then nine and a half years old. The normal school year started in September and finished in June. So by March 1945 I had only three months left to complete the third year of primary school. I was not alone, as the siege of Budapest by the Red Army had interfered with the lives of the whole population. I was enrolled in a state primary school, or rather at two different schools in three months. My continuity of schooling was disrupted when we took off for two weeks to the provinces in order to get some food to make up for the starvation of the previous twelve months.

Mother and I enjoyed visiting Debrecen and Csenger, and swimming in the river Szamos, but friends who accompanied us were devastated by the total extinction of the previous Jewish presence in the villages and towns of Hungary. On our return train journey to Budapest, I recall peasants bringing food to the starving capital, making offensive noises and racial abuse about the bloody Jews, who would not give up their seats to the peasant women, and who were about to go profiteering at the Budapest market. I would have stood up, but my mother refused to let me, another show of extraordinary strength, which made her the person she was. Compared to my mother, saints are a mere bagatelle.

I reported to school after a two-week absence, only to find that school had finished, the pupils had been given their report cards and dismissed. I was devastated; another year out the window. I felt doomed. I was sent alone to the Ministry of Education to ask what was to be done. Feeling desperate, I arrived at the huge building of the Ministry asking to be heard. An elderly gentleman came out, made me sit down and asked what I wanted. I explained the circumstances; he listened and asked me what I had done at school before the holiday. After I had told him, he asked me about thirty questions, and even made me sing a few songs I had learnt. It was the era of Communism in Hungary. All the songs which I had been taught were about the proletarians' Internationale, the partisans, Soviet anthems, songs of the Republic and so on. They may have been anathema to a former royalist ministerial employee, but my educational supervisor did not bat an eyelid. He asked me what I had learnt about religion and history, and the books I had read. At the end he asked me to wait. He went into another office, and returned with an official school report, addressed to me, which was totally unexpected, and left me wondering for weeks afterwards whether anyone could issue such an important document after only talking to me for half an hour, instead of teaching me for a year. The report however was real, and it must have been satisfactory, because in September 1945 I was accepted into fourth year of the primary school at Deák Tér, one of the best schools in Budapest, the so called Lutheran School, which also had a secondary school program highly sought after. My proper education was about to begin.

Year Four at Deák Tér was relatively uneventful. The class comprised forty-two students, all boys, unlike previous schools which were co-educational. We had a regular timetable and an increasingly organised and improved lifestyle in a country ravaged by war. I learnt to keep up with the demands of the school, and came equal or second top of the class, beaten by a boy who had spent some years at the school earlier and was known to the teachers. Decades later I found out from the boy who had been top student, now living in Canada, Dr I. Elkan, that he had returned to Budapest thirty years later and obtained a copy of the computerised school records related to the year we had attended. He knew, unlike me, that he had not come top of the year. From the records, he assured me I came top. We remain close friends.

Secondary Education

The Lutheran School was followed by a change of plan, namely to forego enrolment in the Lutheran high school for the next eight years and to try to be accepted into Trefort (Minta Gimnazium), the university teachers' training school which had a formidable reputation. We had a chance to be enrolled as acceptability hinged on academic scores as well as family background. In terms of the latter, proletarians and the working-class were favoured, so a miner had a better chance than a lawyer of sending his son to a good school. I was regarded as class neutral – mother working, father disappeared in the Holocaust – and I had one further factor in my favour. My mother's uncle was the founding principal of the school, widely revered in teaching circles, still acclaimed a century after his death. I was accepted and subsequently spent three full years at Trefort, an excellent school which prepared me to cope with the future, during which I would be destined to miss another two years of high school education. This school contributed to the education of notable people, such as Edward Teller, Leo Szilard, Lord Balogh and Lord Kaldor amongst others, who fled Hungary before World War Two.

In 1946, my first year at high school, I was introduced to Latin, which I loved. It formed the basis of my interest in languages and expression. Latin was a subject I have studied in three countries, and the three years I spent at Trefort enabled me to sit for Matriculation level in Australia without attending classes, just by copying the notes and spending two days in the public library, doing revision at the end of the year. Students often found Latin tedious and unnecessary. I used to help my friends by doing their homework in class and quickly writing it in their notebook before a lesson. On one occasion I had not finished the translation for my friend before the teacher arrived. The teacher found the incomplete attempt at Latin composition in my friend's notebook, and held it up to show his contempt in front of the class. My work was ridiculed and I was mortified. My friend smiled stoically and kept silent, and I trembled at the thought of being found out. The teacher remained ignorant of the fact that his prize pupil was responsible for a miserable piece of failed homework in somebody else's hands.

History remained my favorite subject; had I followed a humanities course I would have majored in history. As events turned out it was not meant to be, but twenty years later I embarked on a study of British history at university level. I did fairly well and was encouraged to undertake a major in history, but there was a clash between finishing the undergraduate history course or a doctorate in medicine. The M.D. won, but I have never abandoned my fondness for history.

In the second and third years of high school, I was introduced to biology and physics, both of which were taught at a relatively high level, considering that it was only year six and seven of school education. I loved physics, as I thought it was logical, comprehensible and moved along predictable lines, whereas biology was not well taught and it required an extra effort later to pick up its threads in another country. Unfortunately it was not well taught even in Australia. I found it difficult, although at a later date physiology came to complement physics and always remained a firm favorite.

Interestingly, chemistry was not taught at this level in Budapest, and when I first encountered it in Australia, under the name of general science, it was difficult and challenging. Although I tried to cope with it and made it a part of my professional career, it was always the physical chemistry which appealed rather than organic chemistry and the periodic table and its related mysteries.

Mathematics was a subject everybody had to endure, but few students showed any special aptitude in my class. I had never been taught trigonometry and when I encountered that subject later I was totally baffled. I thought it was a branch of mathematics, but how on earth did it come about that whenever we did trigonometry it was all about triangles, and sin, cos and tan and never anything else. It was about forty-five years after leaving school that it suddenly dawned on me that trigonometry was a science of triangles. Why did not anybody tell me this before?

The other subject at Trefort was religious instruction, a carryover from pre-Communist days. It served the purpose mainly of indicating to us who were Jewish and who were converts, as the converts were invariably known to have been Jewish. There was no overt anti-Semitism, except for one teacher who put me down quite blatantly on this basis in Art, but he was dismissed from the school the following year. I later achieved proficiency in Art and my results were helped by the three tins of sardines my mother presented to the new teacher at Christmas time, food being still scarce.

We had Hungarian as a subject. Naturally in all countries the mother tongue is a precious commodity and before the Holocaust I had an admiration for Hungary. But I was a less than enthusiastic student of the language of this country which had just trampled on us. I topped the class, but in transcribing the national anthem for a set piece of homework I did it without looking closely at the original and made the mistake (like most others) of inserting an extra syllable. A meaningless difference, but it blotted my copybook.

Sport was compulsory. We did gym work and I attempted fencing as an extra sport, which I found exhausting and promptly dropped. This revealed my lack of character and questions were asked. In the street we often misbehaved by sneaking up behind other boys and tapping their school bags with ours, causing them to drop them. This was witnessed by the form teacher and a warning was issued, written into the pages of the formal notebook each student had to carry. My family was horrified and I was not given much chance of ever becoming a responsible citizen. But I managed to perform well academically and this helped to wipe out my unworthy conduct.

In 1948–49, my third year of high school, the Communist regime tightened its grip on all aspects of life, including education. The scout movement, previously very popular, was replaced by the Red Pioneer movement. I was never a scout as we could not afford to buy the shirt, necktie and badge. A rich friend's mother offered me her son's discarded trappings, but this offended me deeply as it drew attention to our poor status. I shunned the scouts, but the Pioneers were a more complex proposition. Everybody was encouraged to join the Pioneers. They marched, took part in less-than-spontaneous demonstrations for the Communists, and were bored out of their wits listening to the unadulterated garbage manufactured by the Communist propaganda machine, worshipping the footsteps of the great friend and benefactor of the nation, Comrade Stalin.

If I joined the Pioneers, I could go on doing what I wanted and wag the official Pioneer functions and I would still be *persona grata* on a political level. Alternatively I could refuse to join, and be shunned as a reactionary, and would need to work doubly hard to do half as well academically, as my results would be marked down for being a class enemy. I joined, full of contempt for the system and myself. I knew that we were doing our best to escape from a budding totalitarian tyranny, in a totally discredited country that we detested. I did go to two meetings and attended one other function during the year before we fled. I managed also to get the second- or third-top mark in the class list, in spite of being a less than fully committed Pioneer.

My school education thus far had covered seven years, at the cost of five and a half years of actual tuition. Once we escaped from Hungary we found ourselves totally stripped of all valuables, and on the way to Austria we were subjected to a customs search. Over the border an American aid organisation offered me a scholarship in a distant part of Austria. I could attend school, they would pay for my lodging and give me about eight dollars a month. My mother had to stay in Upper Austria, where she had a job in a refugee camp.

At School in Graz, Austria

So the event I dreaded came to pass. We separated and I was thrown head-first into an Austrian school system with a new language, amongst people I did not know. To start me off, Mother came to Graz with me, charmed the Principal of the V. Bundesrealgymnasium, who accepted me for entry to year eight of the Austrian school system for a temporary spell, period uncertain. I was given the designation *Gastschüler*, guest pupil. There were thirty students, of whom one was of Hungarian origin and spoke to me occasionally. None of the others spoke any language I knew, and I spoke no German. The teachers essentially ignored me, the students could not make me out, I was quiet and tried to catch on. I managed to help them in Latin and English, but the rest was a closed book, and I still have nightmares that I will fail that terrible year eight.

The subjects included geology, which remains a total mystery to this day. The teacher would appear with trays of rocks and ask the students to specify where they came from, what was their composition, how to extract them from the soil, their value, the type of terrain they came from, and so on. I had no idea what we were doing. It could have been ancient Sanskrit. The other subject was geography, never my favourite. The country they naturally concentrated on was Austria, and I had less knowledge or interest in that topic than in American Samoa. The history of the last millennium has not been exactly favourable to my people in this part of Europe, therefore my interest in the subject was less than enthusiastic. Mathematics was incomprehensible. The only subject in which I showed some promise was English, due to four years of previous exposure, coupled with tremendous motivation, in the knowledge that we might one blessed day go to an English-speaking country, wherein lay my future.

However events shaped our lives in unexpected ways. Three months after starting school, a friend from Budapest, who was attending university on an adult fellowship, and I met one of my schoolmates from the Bundesrealgymnasium on the street. A ten-minute conversation followed, and we walked on. Next day in front of all our colleagues in the cafeteria where the refugees habitually dined, my Hungarian friend announced a miracle. He had heard me speak German to a boy from school, and the two of us had chatted in the local dialect, indistinguishable one from one another. I had picked up the language in three months. In later life I was never to use it, but I also never forgot it.

I spent eight months in that school in Graz, and even attempted to take the examination in June 1950 before leaving. I performed very badly, the students barracked for me, and kept telling the examiner to pass me. I did not get a formal document, but I understood tacitly that I had passed in spite of adverse circumstances. I later included this episode in my resume in Australia, in support of my claim for admission to a fantastic school.

One of the incidents I recall from Graz was that a senior student who was taunted by juniors for his fancy suits went around and slapped a number of juniors in the face, very hard. I copped one too. But it was not discriminatory, as he did not know me from a bar of soap. A second memory concerns periods of religious instruction. Austria is almost exclusively Catholic. Most Austrian Jews had been murdered, and many foreign Jews as well, with hundreds of concentration camps dotting the Austrian countryside. I was not going to attend Catholic religious instruction week after week, so after the first few days I had to act. It was acutely embarrassing. I walked out when the young priest with his clerical collar arrived, and subsequently I stayed away from the classroom for the planned period. It would have been easier not to draw attention to myself, but fortunately I was not treated any differently by the class for being different. Only one boy, a Viennese called Höttl, was ever offensive to me, writing racist jibes in his book to taunt me, but I did not respond. Overall I had very fair treatment from the Austrian education system, which shaped my education differently than I would have expected.

What next? After six months learning a trade, or trying to learn the trade of tailoring in readiness for emigration, I left the tailoring workshop, where I was surrounded by two hundred girls. Their confident prediction at my farewell was that 'He will make a good doctor, rather than a dressmaker'. Thank God. This was some prescience. Our next step was to apply for an overseas destination.

Steyr

In Steyr, Upper Austria, we stayed in a camp for refugees, designated as *Flüchtlingslager* (Refugee Camp) 231, on Rooseveltstrasse 6, a remnant of an old Austrian army barracks, with four large, old, ugly two-storey brick buildings and many wooden barracks, with one bathroom for each twenty rooms. In the area in front of the buildings there was a football ground and the whole camp was traversed by unmade roads, deep in mud in autumn and winter, and with poor hygiene and scarce facilities. Successive waves of Jewish dissidents found refuge there after the war, escapees from Poland, Czechoslovakia and Hungary, people with a fright-filled past, and only a dim and uncertain future. Jewish refugees were separated from non-Jews because of traditional anti-Semitic feelings and also because many of the east Europeans had assisted or sympathised with Hitler and hence fled when the Germans were retreating.

In this camp my mother and I had to subsist for fourteen months, waiting for immigration papers from the countries to whom we had applied. This whole process was ludicrous and corrupt. As a war orphan, I was eligible and permitted to enter the United Sates, the Land of the Free, but my mother was ineligible to go there. Canada would have taken her as a domestic servant (with her two diplomas and four languages) because domestic cleaning ladies were needed and the Canadian Government in its wisdom would have classed her in this category. But they would not accept me. They did however accept as a group the whole of the Ukrainian 'Galicia' SS division, with their dependents, about 12,000 people, and settle them in Canada, admittedly at the persuasion of the British Government. This division had been responsible for countless atrocities in the east, including the genocide at Treblinka and Lodz and the Warsaw Ghetto.

Australia was prepared to accept us both, but the problem here was that an official of the Jewish Refugee Aid, working with the International Refugee Organisation, the ubiquitous IRO, sold our landing permit documents to another, more affluent applicant, and thus we lost our place in the queue. As a result our departure was delayed by about six months. We were not overwhelmed with satisfactory offers, so I shall remain forever grateful for the understanding of the Australian Government, which tried to apply some common sense and humanity in keeping families together, and was not just looking after their voters' immediate domestic interests. Australia welcomed us, and we embraced Australia. The love affair continues.

Chapter Nine

A NEW LIFE IN AUSTRALIA

Schooling in Melbourne

After an interregnum of refugee status in Austria, escape from Europe followed. In 1951 my mother and I sailed to a new continent, far away Australia, a wonderful country to which we had been guided by a fateful turn of events. We arrived in Sydney after a five-week sea voyage, having paused and stayed in Melbourne for three days on the way, which was useful in acquainting us with that city. In Sydney, I was enrolled at the local state school, which was in Naremburn close to St. Leonards. As we lived in an immigrant hostel which was crowded and not very enjoyable nor private, we decided to accept an invitation from friends to stay with them in private accommodation in Melbourne. Victoria also appealed more than New South Wales as we had formed the impression that it was more European in character. Sydney's crowds and traffic were also daunting. Even the climate in Melbourne appeared to suit us better. So after four weeks at school in Form Two in Sydney, we arrived in Melbourne and sought advice about the best schools to approach to take me.

Melbourne High was highly recommended but, even in those days in the early 1950s, it was highly selective. I had not attended formal schooling for nine months, between June 1950 and April 1951. Mother took me to Melbourne High School two days after our arrival. The proud castle on the hill, which is an imposing school building to this day, made us apprehensive about the chances of getting me accepted, especially as it was already half way through Term One. What happened next is the most crucial in a series of events in my education, university and higher degrees not excepted. We were told to wait a few minutes while the Headmaster was called. The Headmaster was Brigadier George Langley DSO, a hero of Gallipoli, a commander of the Camel Corps, and the youngest brigadier in the British

Army in World War One. He called us in, made us welcome and I still remember his study from the only time I was there.

He asked us where we came from, and being told we came from Hungary, he asked his secretary to call B. K., a boy in the final year of high school, known as Sixth Form. We talked about my desire to be accepted as a student in the best school in Victoria, as I had always attended the best schools in Hungary and had a report, sadly dated from 1949, two years before. What have I done in the meantime, he asked me. I replied: 'I attended a school in Austria, learnt German and even attempted to take the exams, and passed six subjects. I concentrated on English as I saw that my future was tied to that'.

While we were waiting for the boy who spoke Hungarian to interpret my report from Budapest, we chatted. The Brigadier said that he spoke French and that he was a French teacher. This was providential as my mother spoke French well, as she had studied in Paris, and this fact changed the whole interview. Langley and Mother spent the next hour chatting in French. 'The Brig', as he was affectionately called, had few opportunities to speak with people who spoke French. By the time the secretary found out that B. K. was away with a cold, my fate had been decided – I was accepted.

However the formalities had to be observed. Brigadier Langley asked for John B., also from Budapest, and he promptly appeared. John, who became a lifelong friend, kindly translated the report card relating to my three years of study from Trefort University High School, adding that the school was of the same calibre as Melbourne High, the very best, and I had the marks of a fine student. The Headmaster asked me if I had any papers from the year spent in Austria, and I said I could provide the appropriate documentation next day. I had no problem writing my own report card – a small amount of improvisation was not a problem! (Years later it occurred to me that I was writing a *Schutzpass*, which were also improvised.) Thus the decision was made.

I have been very fortunate with my education. In Australia, as in Hungary and in Austria in later days, my mother was a magician. She always carried the day and achieved the impossible as far as her son's entry to the best schools was concerned.

In Australia we had no money, no income, no patrons, nor high ranking connections. I was able to attend Melbourne High School, the selective boys' school which had the reputation of being as good academically as any of the expensive private schools. So much so that many boys of great promise from wealthy families were sent to this State school, even after obtaining scholarships for entry to private schools. The latter may have had better sporting and entertainment facilities, but they did not have the edge academically, using entry scores to university as the criteria for judging excellence. For many decades I could not get over the fact that in the United States scholarships are available on sporting prowess. Admission to a prestigious university may depend on how fast an individual can run or how skilled he may be with a tennis racket. I still do not equate sports with education or as a university requirement.

Melbourne High School took half of its intake based on residential status, and the other half on previous educational achievements. It catered for students from years nine to twelve. I was permitted to enrol in Year Four, known as 'Intermediate', in reality the tenth year of education, which meant two and a half years of schooling before Matriculation. In effect this would allow me, if I was capable of passing, to finish high school in four years instead of six, with Year Seven in Hungary, and the last three years, Ten to Twelve, in Australia. If it turned out well, I would finish my high school education eight months ahead of when I would have done so in Budapest. This was too good to be true, but it was. As a final comment, the Brigadier said he would place me in a class with no foreigners; he wanted me to become a real Australian. I remain eternally deeply grateful to him and to the school for the next phase of my education, and for the tolerance and rational behaviour that I came to appreciate at Melbourne High School.

The composition of my class was uniform: all working-class boys, all Australian born, with one exception. I had arrived from Europe in April and was plunged into Year Four C amongst the natives, because of the Headmaster's desire to mould me into a good Australian, and 'to stop being a foreigner or a refugee'. I think, from the perspective of many decades later, his idea had considerable merit. It was aided by a remark I grasped fully soon after arrival. During one of the daily recess breaks one of my European friends heard me speak Hungarian and remarked: 'We have an unwritten rule. We never speak any language at school other than English'. This friend, subsequently to become a prominent scientist, is still a friend. I am sure he is not aware of the extent his remark helped me in learning English and adopting it as my 'second mother tongue'. In contrast, some of the boys from the Baltic states, who were linguistically second to none, habitually took every opportunity to speak Latvian whenever two of them met. This became a lifelong habit with many foreigners. They are surprised that I regard this as a failing rather than a bonus when communicating with them. This is especially true as many have forgotten the finer points of their own language without acquiring the refinements of English, either spoken or written.

My introduction to schooling in English was surprisingly pleasant. I noticed no discrimination, I was never bullied, very rarely laughed at, and if so, only by friends. I made many friends from totally different backgrounds, and after a few weeks even brushed aside the occasional person who, thinking that a new environment could be difficult, tried to assist me. I loved and continue to hold Melbourne High School high in my affections.

My form had, apart from me, only one 'foreigner', and he was English. It became clear that being English was a greater barrier to being accepted than being a total linguistic and ethnic stranger. My English friend, who was very clever, was nicknamed 'Whizzer' after a comic book character. His family was prominent, his father being head of one of the major charitable organisations. In spite of this he was never accepted as an Aussie. It may have been an individual, idiosyncratic trait which prevented him from acting as childishly as most of the boys in the class, or his accent, rather supercilious and very British in manner, may have been a barrier. This boy sat next to me for a year, and we became fairly close, but I sensed he felt somewhat superior to the others, including myself. Many years later I heard that he had returned to Britain and become editor of one of the most prestigious English political weeklies. My assessment that he liked Australia much less than I did seemed to be proved correct.

As the Headmaster intended, it was not the Europeans who accepted me, but the Australians. On one occasion when the larrikins of the class tried to attack me, the form captain Herb Beveridge, who was a tremendous person, put them firmly in their place. My teachers were terrific, especially my mathematics teacher. He was an elderly man called back from retirement, and he realised the difficulties I faced with the interruptions to my schooling. He helped me a great deal, aided by another family friend, a physicist. This man, who gave me private coaching in mathematics, later went to Princeton University to become a designer of the lunar module for the historic Apollo space mission. Starting with the result of thirty-three percent in mathematics in Term One, at the end of the year I received a satisfactory pass mark and a laudatory report, which went to my head. The following year I was less distinguished, but two years later in Year Twelve, Matriculation, I managed to do well, was awarded a scholarship and entered Medicine. This caused a great deal of joy to my mother, and I hope she would have approved of my subsequent progress.

The Years of Distress

In October 1953, in the middle of preparing for Matriculation exams, my mother announced that she was to go for a week's holiday to Sydney. It was characteristic of her altruism and overwhelming care for me that she would tell a white lie, to spare me the agony of the truth. A week earlier she had been diagnosed with cancer of the breast. She was a pessimist, or in this case a realist, and she knew it meant a death sentence. She delayed the decision to have anything done, or rather she had delayed the original decision to go to a doctor for an assessment, in order to spare me anxiety and avoid interfering with my preparations for Matriculation, the final year of high school, which was, and still remains, the most important career-related test of the school system. Its results determine eligibility and scholarships for entry to university, including Medicine, which I was resolved to attempt.

Mother sought the opinion of a European-trained surgeon practising in Melbourne, because she was convinced that European doctors were the best, and then she went for a vacation without telling me any details. By the time she returned, my exams were over. She came back mutilated, in pain after a radical mastectomy, never to regain that sense of joie de vivre, energy, and vitality which characterised her previous personality, infused by her hopes for our future in Australia. She never worked full time again. She was able to earn only a meagre income working as a finisher for a clothing company, doing hand-made adjustments to blouses and pullovers from her sick bed for the next few years. I worked during vacation before the start of the university term. Once employed by a wealthy supermarket magnate, under the supervision of his ancient gardener to restore the grounds of his palatial house, I was asked to cut down trees, clear shrubs, move plants and dig up earth. It was heavy manual labour, and made me strong and physically fit.

During the academic year I worked for periods in business offices as a clerk and also as a waiter, always with the horrible thought at the back of my mind that Mother was critically ill. She was never free from the pain caused by bone metastases. She had seen many doctors who tried to tell her she was cured and she was imagining the pain. I believed that doctor's tale, because I wanted to believe it. In retrospect it is agonising to recall that she was given psychotherapy and even electric shock treatment for what was at the time the incredulity of the medical profession, with their lack of techniques for diagnosing pain and willingness to attribute it to depression.

There was a major blemish yet to come in my academic career. 1954 was a year best forgotten. In my first year at university, Mother's illness caused me terrible stress. I tried to bury my head in the sand and not face the possibility of her failing to recover. I did far less study than I should have, given the difficulty of passing the medical course at a very demanding university. It was a period of growing up, sadness, worry, coupled with irresponsibility. I did not work well, and did not try to excel, and failed under circumstances which still seem outrageous. Out of a pre-med class of 215 students, normally about 70 percent were expected to pass. That year however the figure was closer to 45 percent. One reason was political pressure to abolish quotas, for the intake into second year was gaining momentum and many students, especially returned soldiers who had passed first year, but not sufficiently well to gain entry into second year, were clamouring to be admitted. It was decided to fail a higher proportion of the first year intake than customary, to make way for the banking up of earlier candidates.

The second reason was that a particularly obnoxious lecturer called Brown, universally detested by the students, took offence at some minor disturbance of marbles being rolled down his lecture theatre. He took a vindictive delight in setting an inappropriately difficult examination paper, not normally offered to medical students but to science students, causing an enormous number of the medical group to fail. The margin of failure was only two or three marks and most students were denied a supplementary examination, and so were forced to repeat the whole year. Those who failed that year included about thirty members of the class, many of whom subsequently became professors of medicine, surgery and psychiatry, and well-known medical consultants.

During the year I played cards and chased girls, but not to the degree that I deserved to fail. It is difficult to describe this unexpected and serious event. In November 1954, looking at the university notice board with the results displayed, I experienced the shock of feeling like a criminal, because I had failed with no right of appeal. I felt I should die, facing my desperately ill Mother, who had devoted her life to helping me to do medicine, and whom I had wantonly betrayed. To this day I have never forgiven myself for this awful lapse. An older man, Andrew Varigos, a wonderful colleague at the university, took me home and tried to put a good face to the blow, which threatened – in fact came within a whisker – of ending my medical ambitions. I had missed only one subject by a few marks. I admitted my errors to an advisor to the welfare society which supported my mother, and I was trusted when I promised to make amends. Fortunately, and perhaps aware of the injustice committed by Brown and the politics of playing with the futures of potentially talented people, the university permitted some students to repeat the year, and even excused them from needing to attend subjects they had already passed.

The Remainder of My Course

I was one of those allowed to re-enrol, this time however without my Commonwealth Scholarship of £42 every three months, amounting to about £2.15 shillings per week, which was enough income for me to go to the university. Very rich distant relatives offered to help me to become an assistant in a retail pharmacy. I slammed the phone on them and henceforth spoke of them in terms unfit to record. The following year I did not miss one class, and worked on each day's new material on the same night and for a few nights afterwards. I developed a successful technique of not taking any notes in lectures, instead writing out the whole lecture immediately afterwards from memory. This was the basis of subsequent techniques of learning, teaching and planning scientific projects.

During the repeat year, I was working ever more frequently in odd jobs and got very tired, but my mother was confident I would succeed and she was more stable than earlier, having received deep X-ray and hormone therapies, quite advanced for the era. The treatments however had side effects, of which she was painfully aware. She received wonderful support from Dr Stoll, head of radiotherapy at the Peter McCallum Hospital, who recognised me thirty years afterwards at a meeting where I received a cancer therapy award. He spoke warmly of my mother, whom he remembered well. His help at the time of her terminal illness was a major factor in keeping our fragile existence going.

The year ended well, as I managed to get honours, regained my scholarship, and never failed again, nor showed lack of effort. The following year was very difficult. Mother had a lot of pain and disability through years of being misdiagnosed as having an emotional illness. We studied together – I remember reading my anatomy textbook early in the mornings, going to her room, handing her the book, *Gray's Anatomy*, reciting the relevant topic and receiving corrections. I also decided to learn French. Mother loved France, especially Paris, and the culture and language of the French, and taught me enough in those few months for me to build on that initial learning later, when living in Paris and during my numerous trips to France. My discovery of relatives in Paris was a major source of pleasure in later years.

By the end of 1956 I had received significant moral support from the university, to the extent that my frequent compulsory absences because of my mother's illness were excused. After the annual examinations I was offered the chance of telling her my favourable results, via a confidential message sent to her by the Registrar of the Medical Faculty, days before the official publication of results. But the summer of 1956–57 was tinged with sadness – the diagnosis of bony secondaries was finally confirmed. A kind family friend made it possible for me to be employed working from home on documents related to his engineering business so that I was spared any separation from her during the last summer of her life.

My mother was wasted but retained her intellect and wonderful courage to the last. In 1957 she underwent further procedures to supplement her hormone-related treatment, and for a period of eight weeks she was pain free. Her passing in September 1957 brought my world to an end. Anything that has ever happened to me since is really the second volume of my life, not part of my original existence, and not associated with her physical presence, but associated with her memory and spiritual presence, more strongly than ever almost six decades later.

The devastation of my mother's death was indescribable. Work saved me and friends helped, which I have never forgotten. I threw myself into studies after missing the original dates or failing. Given special considerations on compassionate grounds, the university decided to grant me supplementary examinations. Brilliant teaching from exceptionally gifted friends enabled me, after four weeks, to pass the most demanding year of the medical course. I then enrolled in the fourth year. For twelve months I was in mourning, deeply and profoundly depressed. Studying was a lifeline with its own rewards. When I finished the medical course I was the only student from my clinical school to gain honours in Medicine, the major subject. I had made it.

A Gifted Colleague

I did not make it, however, on my own.

Australian school years have been traditionally divided into three terms, with examinations at the end of each term. One year after the second term examinations at Melbourne High, my class kept muttering about another, parallel class composed of an international set of brilliant students from all over Europe. There was a particular boy with a European name, not Jewish, possibly French, who was a subject of admiration and envy. Already in Year Ten he had performed so brilliantly that he was said to have been 'recommended for exemption' from taking the third term examination in most subjects. Not until Year 11 did I have the opportunity to meet Georges. We both chose the Science/Medicine stream and were placed in the same class, mainly because of the timetable involving biology. Biology was not a pre-requisite for Medicine, but students were advised take it if they intended to study Medicine. Georges took advanced mathematics, namely applied maths and calculus, plus pure maths. I did general maths, which was considerably easier. We were in separate English classes, but shared physics and chemistry classes.

Very soon, within days, I realised that the legend was true. Georges was quite astonishingly gifted and exceptionally versatile. Totally matter of fact and unpretentious in behaviour, his grasp of concepts was phenomenal. He was able to solve a series of fifty mathematics questions, set as a trial examination for the term, overnight. In a comparable time, others managed to struggle through two or three of the questions, and I belonged to that group. Georges could look at a problem, start writing, and complete the answer in minutes, with startling logic. He had a self-admitted photographic memory, and could 'read things off the page in his mind's eye'. This however was only a tool. There are many people with photographic memory who are not brilliant thinkers and don't have the ability to produce answers to specific questions requiring multiple sources of information. Georges had a gift for all the above.

What he did at school continued for the rest of his life. He was able to listen to a lecture, produce copious notes, and then present the data in such a manner that it vastly eclipsed the original presentation of experienced lecturers. He did this with a predictable regularity in all subjects at all levels of perceived difficulty. It did not appear to matter if the original presentation was sub-standard, the lecturer had a poor delivery, his material was old, badly prepared or deficient. Notes taken by Georges were guaranteed to be better than a textbook – outstanding models of clarity and simplicity. He was equally at home with biology or English; he was editor of the school magazine, excellent in French, and totally unassuming, almost embarrassingly modest. He kept referring to his brother as the real intellect, much brighter than himself, and gave credit to other people for the least amount of wit or sparkle exhibited on a single occasion. Georges was a stunning looking, charismatic person, tall and slim with brown curly hair, deep blue eyes, a clear confident voice, and a personality to match. He was universally admired and respected, attracting women like bees flocking to honey. His friends were legion and he assisted those in need while remaining undemanding and modest to a fault.

Georges subsequently became a knowledgeable and practical doctor, an excellent resident and winner of the highest university distinction after obtaining his higher doctorate. I have never known a detractor or enemy who regarded himself as such, and interest in his progress continues five decades after his disappearance – partly as a result of a possible illness, but more likely self-imposed. Georges came from a humble background. His father died young from diabetic complications with his mother bringing him up with the help of scholarships.

He was generous with his time, gave instructions freely and brilliantly. Such was the confidence engendered by his teaching that he was implicitly trusted, and what he thought important was invariably the crux of any discussion, and was accepted by his peers. In year eleven he was exempted again from all final tests, and at Matriculation he won the highest aggregate in the state. He won high first class honours in two branches of mathematics, physics, and biology, and a general exhibition. He was not interested in sports and decided he would study nuclear physics at university, making a full sweep of the first-year science prizes. He did so well that, as the results had to be standardised, he was marked out of two hundred to give anyone else a chance of passing.

Georges decided to switch to Medicine, but continued to enrol in second year science subjects plus biology, which was obligatory for entry to second year medicine. He again topped his year, including biology, although he could not attend a single lecture, as lecture times had clashed with the mathematics lectures. From then on we were in the same class. He collected all the medicine prizes, apart from two individual subjects. His assignments and examination papers in biochemistry were circulated as examples of perfect answers.

It was during third year, in the most difficult part of the medical course, that my mother died and I failed all subjects. I recall sitting in the Union building cafeteria in 1957, almost sixty years ago, when the prizes were announced. Georges had won the Anatomy Prize, including the Embryology and Histology Prizes, plus top awards in Physiology and Biochemistry, and other major prizes. I was delighted for him and, suddenly, I shuddered as though I had been struck by lightning. I could not believe I had not thought of this before. 'I am going to get Georges to coach me for the supplementary examinations awarded to me in view of special circumstances'.

I had to take these exams in twenty days. My thought was that as Georges had finished studying and would be free, and as I was in desperate need, he would help me. I needed to hurry and ask him, in case he had taken a vacation job. This was probably the greatest single idea I ever had in my life. I say this six decades later, with full cognisance of what it means.

Georges was already committed. He had a job working in a factory at a salary of £12 per week. I put my proposition to him: 'I'll pay you £15, you do not need to leave home, normal working hours, five days a week, I shall come to you, and all we need is your genius, my commitment and total concentration.' He accepted instantaneously. We did exactly as planned for three weeks, coached by the greatest intellect whom I or anyone else who ever knew him had ever encountered. A delight. After doing some trial questions, I was told by Georges to take two days off before the tests and have confidence. The examination was memorable. Whenever in doubt about a question, I paused and wondered what Georges would do. The answers came thick and fast. I passed without any hint of doubt or difficulty. I considered it a triumph of Georges's teaching. I still do.

Subsequently we became very close friends. He was always available to help or clarify any academic problems. On a social level we enjoyed that last three years of the medical course in the company of a close-knit group of friends. Georges became the Dux of the final year of the Medical Course, with such a margin that his aggregate of eighty-five percent was followed by three categories of 'no candidate'. He beat the second placegetter by eight percent of the total marks, a phenomenal margin. After graduation, resident and registrar posts and higher degrees followed.

Then something went wrong. He lost interest in his profession, became involved with astrology, parapsychology and numerology, dropped out of medicine and enrolled to do a Ph.D., but failed to finish it. I remember him saying he 'did not want to be a laboratory person, removed from real life'. He began to shun his friends, and although all who knew him were distressed, none could offer help, because, as someone put it succinctly 'he is so much brighter than any of us, who are we to press our opinion on him?' Subsequently, after a gap of ten years, he decided to resume his studies in mathematics. He attended Sydney University and took the examination, doing so brilliantly that he had to be marked again out of two-hundred percent to permit anyone else to pass.

At the hospital where he worked for five years, the consultant staff were concerned about his progress. Georges became a subject of endless discussions. Although we knew his ancestry, senior people at the hospital obviously did not. We had heard from Georges that his grandparents included a defrocked French priest, a Swedish sea-captain, an English and an Irish grandmother, but that his parents were born in Australia. The surgeons at the hospital seemed to know better. One of them said Georges was a brilliant man, that he was of Danish origin, whose parents came to Australia when he was a child. Clearly a figment of imagination, as his school friends well recognised. But the name stuck. From that day onwards, Georges acquired the nickname 'Dane', still used by his close friends.

He disappeared from our horizon in the 1970s and resisted all attempts to renew contact. His mother died in about 1978. At a reunion of graduates from school, I was talking to people I had not met for forty years and when they asked me about Georges I told them what little I knew. Moving to the next table, I was immediately asked by another group: 'What happened to Georges?' Finally someone else, now working as a statistician, replied sadly: 'I heard he died, but I cannot confirm it.' In light of more recent evidence it seems Georges is alive, but apparently unable to re-join his devoted friends. There will never be an equal to him. His towering intellect is clearly mirrored in the final results of that medical course years ago and all his other intellectual triumphs. A man about whom all his peers proudly proclaim: 'The brightest man ever.'

Chapter Ten

MY LATER MEDICAL CAREER

An Intern Year

I had graduated with honours in Medicine, a high point of my life, and I knew I would try to pursue a career as a physician. Naively I thought I had started on that road, but little did I expect that my education was about to commence once more. Medicine is largely a practical profession, and although it was not compulsory at the time I graduated, resident or intern years were expected to follow graduation. Further studies and academic tests leading to higher degrees were not encouraged until the third or fourth postgraduate year. In the first two years after graduation the time spent in learning the practical issues of managing patients overrode any thoughts of sitting down reading books. While working as an intern it was regarded as a blessed opportunity even to have a cigarette or to take a break during rostered hours off duty. The period of work sometimes amounted to about 150 hours on call a week. Only one night off a fortnight, and two evenings off a week, with a return to duty by midnight on evenings off.

This tremendous workload served to expose a new doctor to the demands of practice, but its effect was more like turning graduates off general medicine. They wished for the day they could either leave the hospital with its regimentation, or climb up the ranks to more bearable levels of employment. In order to progress to these higher levels, such as specialties, consultant posts, or academic employment, further study was involved, which in my case continued for many decades. My first aim was to get a Doctorate in Medicine (MD), a higher degree, which was not encouraged at the clinical school where I had studied. I recall a conversation with one of my seniors, who said to me; 'Why study for an MD – who wants to be an academic? I want to be real doctor'. How wrong he was. Without having the foresight to do a thesis, he would never learn the discipline needed to organise research, and would end up as a busy 'real doctor', such as a jobbing physician.

I started studying for the MD ahead of the College diploma, although the normal progression was to get the physician's qualification out of the way before embarking on a university controlled doctorate. The first part required passing an examination, which I failed. I was successful in the written, but failed the oral examination, which was a knife-edge affair, where some candidates were clearly favoured by the choice of venues and the patients selected to be used for the examination. It was held on that occasion at another hospital, and the local candidates had seen all the patients who were chosen to be examined. Unfair? Many thought so. Reluctantly I joined the queue of those hoping to become candidates for membership of the College of Physicians.

Further Study in the United Kingdom

I was so disillusioned that, rather than spend a further year in Melbourne as a registrar, I sailed for England in 1965, intending to see the world, and to take the London examination for the Membership of the College of Physicians which operated under a different, multiple choice system of examination. I entered the appropriate details on the College forms, paid the fee, which was not excessive, and received notification that the examination would take place in October. In London I received additional coaching for the membership examination by the late Dr Pappworth, who took classes composed mainly of overseas aspirants; his intelligent teaching deserved the highest credit. I failed, and could not believe it, after passing the Australian written exam, which was more advanced, because it closely corresponded to a second stage of the British test. I decided to re-sit in three months, and in the meantime applied for the test for Scottish Membership of the Royal College of Physicians of Edinburgh (MRCP Ed.). (Many years later this diploma was joined with the London diploma, to become the membership of Colleges of Physicians of the United Kingdom.)

While in Edinburgh from June 1965 onwards, friends took me sightseeing and to see a Gilbert and Sullivan opera. The food in Edinburgh was vastly superior to that in London, and at prices I could afford. My chosen field for the Edinburgh membership was Neurology, my favourite area of medicine, in which I had received training in my last post in Australia by Dr Arthur Schwieger. I duly undertook two three-hour written papers in general medicine and in neurology. I then faced the formidable hurdle of oral examinations involving two long cases, which I remember most vividly, at separate times and in different locations. Later I was examined on several short cases, pathology specimens, and electrocardiographs. There were also several theoretical vivas, which were conducted in various hospitals. The general medical examination was held in Glasgow. The College gave me a half crown to pay for the train ticket, which I cherished and still have to this day.

The patient I was examining for the exam had multiple problems, including jaundice and a cardiac lesion, probably mitral stenosis. I was able to make the correct diagnoses, in spite of immense difficulties in coping with the Glasgow accent. In later years, talking about language, I lightheartedly said that I could not understand a word the patient spoke. This is an exaggeration, but I think I passed the examination by simply reporting the findings and the subsequent discussion. The long neurological case was held in Edinburgh. I was the last candidate, as my name was alphabetically at the end of the list of the candidates to be examined. Professor John Marshall, a famous Edinburgh neurologist, who was working at Queen's Square in London at the time, was my examiner.

There were several factors in my favour. The examination was very tiring for both examiner and candidate, and as the examinations were running late, I had over an hour to think about my case, whereas the examiners were exhausted by the morning's work. I had a very sympathetic supervisor, the person who introduced the candidates, who asked me: 'Is there any relation between the two lesions you have discovered?' I said 'No', and he replied 'That's right.' This exchange gave me boundless confidence. The patient had motor neurone disease and a thyroid lesion, and I managed to have a sensible approach on to how to manage these. The short cases and vivas went well, except when I was confronted by two neurosurgeons at the last hurdle, who quizzed me about cerebrospinal fluid dynamics, a question I apparently failed to answer correctly on the written paper and probably also on the oral.

I was so sure I had failed; I was mortified and decided that it was the end of my academic career. I did not attend the publication of results, nor the farewell function, booked my ticket and bought two books to read on the train. One of them was *A Singular Man*, by J.P. Donleavy, which caused me to laugh all to way back to London. The other book was *Catch-22*, by Joseph Heller, which also achieved great acclaim and was later made into a film. Feeling my path to specialisation in medicine was over I was resigned and miserable. Then a telegram arrived from a friend in Edinburgh: 'Passed'. I was so overjoyed I embraced and passionately kissed the elderly Nigerian lady who delivered the telegram. Passing was a tremendous boost for my future as it was the first of my higher degrees. Never since have I received such fabulous news, with the exception of the birth of our son. I took several minutes each time I signed my name, to put MRCP (Ed) prominently, and with great pride, at the end of my signature. The Edinburgh Membership exam was the most valuable path in opening up my medical career and I thank the College, humbly, for making it possible.

Back in Australia

In spite of getting the qualification, Queen's Square Hospital, where I had been taught as a visitor, would not respond favourably to my application for a job. This disappointment was compounded by the fact that I was informed that there was no room in Melbourne for another neurologist. At that time there were about eight practicing neurologists – now we have about 250 – a strange perspective on what was required. On my return I took the examination for Membership of the Royal Australian College of Physicians (MRACP); holding the Scottish qualification made it much easier for me in Australia. Not that College examiners are limited in their horizons, but they had a tendency to follow a set pattern: once someone else made a decision, it was acceptable to repeat it. Next came a series of jobs and attempting a Doctorate of Medicine (MD). I had not given up the quest for this degree and wanted to become in my eyes a 'serious doctor', not to give up patient care, but to do something original and problem oriented, rather than making medical practice like a trade or industry.

In order to devote my full attention to the MD, I gave up my course in Arts, majoring in History. This could have been my first love, but I felt the MD was going to be of more long-term value. This was correct, but I still regret not pursing history further. I also relinquished learning French privately because of the pressure of time. Fortunately I was appointed to a professorial assistant position and given a MD topic. I turned to academia and was fortunate to be supported by Dr Roger Mellick, a great physician, and Dr T.J. Martin, later a Fellow of the Royal Society, to start a project in Endocrinology, which turned out to be rewarding. Subsequently I worked under Professor R. Lovell and contributed to the first controlled clinical trial assessing the risk of sudden death after heart attacks. I received my Doctorate after completing a thesis, comparable to a Ph.D. (I think it was an atrocious decision by Melbourne University in 2010 to abolish the MD degree or, worse still, make it a graduate qualification, as in the US. It was one of the most highly regarded degrees, pursued by almost all medical academics for the past seventy years.)

Pharmacology and Neurology

After Melbourne I returned in January 1972 to Britain for three years in the pursuit of pharmacology, therapeutics and the pleasures of London. I trained in Clinical Pharmacology at the Hammersmith Hospital under Professors Colin Dollery and Alaisdare Breckenridge, subsequently both Knights of the Realm. It was a most instructive and enjoyable period in my medical career, working in an environment where every single colleague was brighter than I was, and taught me a lot about pharmacology. After a post at London University in Clinical Pharmacology at the Middlesex Hospital, I came back to Melbourne, was appointed to the Austin Hospital as a neurologist by Professors Austin Doyle and W.J. Louis, and embarked on a career liaising between neurology and pharmacology. I have worked with my iconic friend Dr Peter Bladin, who made the Neurology Department at the Austin one of the major medical centres in Australia, with some brilliant students, later highly honoured leaders of the profession, such as Drs Sam Berkovic, and Geoff Donnan. My own education continued, as I developed a pattern of writing up research endeavours and editing proceedings of scientific meetings. I received frequent invitations to speak on the scientific data I was researching. All this comprised further education, not to speak of supervising candidates for higher degrees, whom I had the pleasure to work with.

In Stockholm in 1992 I married Michele Watson, who was a nurse at the Alfred Hospital, and now manages my small neurology practice. We have a son, Simon Raoul Leslie, born in 1987, who after matriculating (now a politically incorrect term) at my old school, Melbourne High, went on to a Performing Arts degree at Monash University, and later computer science at Swinburne. The birth of our son, who bears the three first names of Raoul Wallenberg, Simon Wiesenthal and my martyred Father, testifies to the memory of those people and my resolve to fight racist oppression. My wife Michele has given unstinting support in these endeavours and my son has brought unparalleled joy to my life, and as I always put it, Simon Raoul Leslie has provided a new dimension to our lives.

In 1988 I resigned from the Austin, and in order to earn a living after leaving there participated in evaluations of new drugs for the Therapeutic Administration in Canberra. I continue to have good relations with the pharmaceutical industry, which has supported me over many years. In 1994 I was invited by Professor Ed Byrne, the Director of Neurosciences, to join him at St Vincent's Hospital, my old Alma Mater, and was appointed as Senior Principal Neurologist. I also established the Australian Register of

Epilepsy and Pregnancy, currently in its fifteenth year, which collected data from 2500 women afflicted with a seizure disorder. I am particularly indebted to St Vincent's and in particular to Professor James Best, for their support.

In 1995 it was suggested by Professor Byrne that I ought to set up an Australian Centre for Clinical Neuropharmacology at the hospital to undertake research into drugs used in neurology. The original meeting was orchestrated by Professor Byrne in conjunction with Professor Mervyn Eadie, the doyen of clinical neuro-pharmacologists in Australia, who spoke eloquently about the need for such an initiative. Twelve pharmaceutical companies joined in a consortium to support the Centre, which has since conducted a number of research projects. The official opening was performed by the Governor of Victoria, Sir James Gobbo.

Further Appointments

In 2004 I was invited by Professor Richard Larkins, Vice Chancellor of Monash University, and Ed Byrne, by then the Dean of Medicine, to come to Monash to continue my research as Professor of Clinical Neuropharmacology. For many years this has involved compiling a register of anti-epileptic drug exposure in pregnant women with epilepsy. This work has been carried out in affiliation with overseas colleagues, amongst whom I am particularly grateful for the support of Emilio Perucca from Pavia, Torbjorn Tomson from Sweden, and Dina Battino from Milan. I continue to publish on neurological and pharmacological topics, my main interest being in epilepsy and neurodegenerative disease. Collaboration with Mervyn Eadie, Cecilie Lander and Terence O'Brien yielded a great track record of results, which is a credit to the team. Janet Graham as research coordinator established herself as an invaluable asset to this research. Amongst other colleagues, I had great support from Stephen Davis and Fred Mendelssohn, as well as many of my former students and researchers, who have risen to great heights professionally.

After four years at Monash, Professor Terence O'Brien, one of my most brilliant students, invited me to come to the Royal Melbourne Hospital, where work continues in collaboration with the European International Register, based in Milan and Stockholm. Professor Mervyn Eadie, former Head of the Department of Neurology in Brisbane, and I, co-edited *The Handbook of the Clinical Pharmacology of Antiepileptic Drugs*, as well as producing about fifty joint publications on pregnancy and epilepsy-related issues. In 2007, while at Monash, I received the Peter Bladin Award for contributions to epilepsy research. In 2012 I was honoured by the Governor General with Membership of the Order of Australia for contributions to epilepsy, neuropharmacology and services to the Jewish community.

I now live in Kew, and continue to work in part-time academic medicine and practice. Overseas travel and presentations at conferences have become part of my life, but are now less frequent. I have about 350 publications including books, chapters in books, major articles plus abstracts, mostly in collaboration with colleagues. My deep thanks are due to all those mentioned and many other colleagues not listed by name. In a book of this size I hope that these pages on my medical contributions do not appear excessive, but they may serve to indicate that I have been busy.

In later years further honorary degrees followed, but I think the accolades matter less than personalising material, or opening up new fields of endeavour. The process is lifelong, or as long as one is able to work and contribute. This can only be judged by publications, by the success of students at gaining their diplomas, and by performing at high levels. The story told here could appropriately be called my schooling; my education continues and will do so indefinitely. The details of the final examination will not be determined by earthly examiners.

PART TWO

*RAOUL WALLENBERG ...
AS I REMEMBER*

Chapter Eleven

RAOUL WALLENBERG IN HUNGARY

The date was 12 March 1982. In my bedroom just before retiring in the evening, the late television news had just ended. I suddenly looked at the screen, awestruck. The announcer went on:

> And suddenly a young man climbed on the top of the cattle trucks and opened the doors, calling out names and offering protection papers – he called them *Schutzpasses* – to the people who reached out eagerly to grab them. This young man was Raoul Wallenberg, employed by the Swedish Embassy, whose mission was to rescue as many Jews as possible from the clutches of the German Nazis and their odious Hungarian collaborators. The armed guards fired shots over his head, but he did not flinch and would not leave until he accomplished his task for the moment, and left with a handful of condemned Jews, who were temporarily freed from the imminent threat of deportation to the gas chambers at Auschwitz.

This news item changed my life.

The announcer was giving a preview of a television documentary to be shown the following Saturday: 'The Righteous Gentile, Raoul Wallenberg, who was the rescuer of tens of thousands of Hungarian Jews, who may possibly be alive even now, languishing in Soviet captivity.' My whole being was transformed. I knew that moment that I had just heard one of the most personally relevant announcements I was to hear in my life.

Raoul Wallenberg was about to be discussed openly in the West in terms of the recognition he deserved. Perhaps this documentary might shed light on the fate of the man to whom I owed my life, the leader who sought to rescue an entire population at a time when they were about to be slaughtered. That night I could not sleep. I continued to discuss with great excitement the event due next weekend, and prepared two video-recorders to capture the film. I watched it, mesmerised, as, in the truly British understated manner, the documentary recounted the events of 1944: the hardships, horrors and

Wallenberg's accomplishments. I took careful note of all the witnesses, noted the tone of relative optimism about Wallenberg's possible survival, and feverishly planned a way to participate in the inevitable explosion of interest in the Wallenberg case.

Like a born-again believer, I knew my role was to be an advocate for the justice that had eluded Wallenberg, and that I must devote my energies to his cause, above all other interests or obligations. I have spent as much time on the Wallenberg issue as on my other professional and personal commitments. In retrospect, three decades later, I am confident in saying that nothing else has provided me with so much personal satisfaction as having Wallenberg's name become a symbol for human courage, not only in Australia but in other parts of the world.

Immediately after watching the BBC documentary *Man Alive – Missing Hero*, by John Bierman, I attempted to establish contact with other survivors from Budapest to form a Wallenberg Committee in Australia or to join an existing one. I was only partly successful in this attempt, as most people could not understand my burning sense of urgency and failed to put me in touch with those who participated in the film. Fortunately, a few days later a close friend presented me with John Bierman's book, *Raoul Wallenberg: Righteous Gentile*, upon which the TV documentary had been based. The author, whom I met some years later, was a BBC journalist, who had travelled extensively to interview Budapest Jews concerned with Wallenberg's disappearance and fate.

I recall I had such an urgency to act that I did not simply read the book, but as soon as I read a sentence I translated it into Hungarian, with a view to publishing it, naively thinking that if it were disseminated amongst those who owe their lives to Wallenberg, there may be a sudden swelling in the outcry for his release. In the event I completed the translation, writing by hand, in fourteen days, and while this was going on I wrote to John Bierman asking for a right to translate. The reply, slow in arriving, referred me to his agent, who was fairly distant and non-committal. I stated Bierman could have all the proceeds of the Hungarian edition, but in spite of this his agent tried to discourage me. It would have taken more than a literary agent or a British journalist to dampen my interest.

I wrote immediately to Stockholm, addressing my letter to the Wallenberg Association and placing my enthusiasm at their disposal. That same week I read about the Australian Union of Jewish Students holding a rally in support of Wallenberg, and forming a Free Wallenberg Committee here. I attended the rally, held at the Beth Weizmann Hall in the presence of Rabbi Abraham Cooper, who was on a lecture tour co-ordinating the fight for

Raoul Wallenberg. Cooper said he wished I would do more than translate the Bierman book, as the Wallenberg movement was in need of creative ideas, to which I might contribute. He presented me with another book on Wallenberg, this one written by Elenore Lester: *Wallenberg: The Man in the Iron Web*.

After the meeting, a television crew interviewed the participants, and I was asked for comments. This was my first television interview and I did not mince words:

> The kidnapping and detention of Raoul Wallenberg by the Soviet Union is the most appallingly brutal and cynical exercise in duplicity. It is so abhorrent that until Wallenberg is released I refuse to regard the Russians as my liberators, even though it was the Red Army who ultimately saved me from the Nazi murderers. I vow that I shall devote every ounce of energy to trying to liberate Raoul and shirk from no effort to do so.

This interview was duly reported in Melbourne and made me rather hesitant to go to Hungary or the Soviet Union ever again, as I felt the KGB would not look kindly on people who protested strongly about Soviet duplicity and breaches of international law. With my feelings toward my birthplace being tinged with revulsion and contempt, I had no desire to revisit Budapest, even after the fall of Communism. Soon after the rally I received a letter from Raoul Wallenberg's sister, who expressed her appreciation for my interest, hoped that I would continue to exert myself in Raoul's behalf, and wished for his eventual release. This letter, which I cherish to this day, sealed my plan to become a fighter in the Wallenberg cause.

In my library I have a cutting from *Time* magazine in late 1979, which gives a summary of what were believed to be the circumstances of Wallenberg's arrest and subsequent captivity in the Gulag. It stated that President Reagan was interested in the case and was going to make approaches to the Soviets. This brief report was the only written piece of information I had ever come across on Raoul Wallenberg since 1945, except for repeatedly passing down the street named after him in Budapest. Each time I paused and felt deeply downcast about the injustice done to this man who disappeared after the war, rumoured to be have been taken by the Russians as an alleged spy, or possibly killed by the Fascists.

Wallenberg's Early Career

In 1979 at a conference aimed at discussing the Wallenberg issue in Stockholm, Simon Wiesenthal said that it was our duty to fight for Raoul Wallenberg's release, not only as Jews, but as free human beings fighting for a man who did so much for human dignity. Fighting for Wallenberg was even more important than bringing Nazi war criminals to justice, and we all know that Wiesenthal had devoted his life to the latter. For those people who survived the Holocaust in Budapest the name of Raoul Wallenberg has been a constant source of gratitude, and can still evoke emotional outbursts of grief for the loss of our families, and for the fate of the man who may have achieved more in six months than all the underground armies of Europe in saving a significant portion of a Jewish population in the hell of Nazi-occupied Hungary. Though a hero to all the survivors of the Hungarian Jewry, Wallenberg remained less well known to the rest of the world.

For this reason when one spoke to an audience in the 1980s, it was necessary to sketch the details of who Raoul Wallenberg was and what he did. Fortunately these days his story is better known; there are streets, parks and monuments that bear his name, he has been an Honorary Citizen of the United States, Canada and Israel for three decades, there are many books and films about him, and he has been the subject of countless articles, speeches and tributes worldwide, being regarded as one of the foremost of the Righteous Gentiles, the men and women who risked their lives to save Jews. His tree in the Yad Vashem Holocaust memorial centre was planted by the Prime Minister of Israel later than many of the others, as Raoul's family did not wish to imply that he was dead and instead waited for his return. Renewed awareness of Wallenberg over the past decades was sparked in part by a 1980 *New York Times* article by Elenore Lester, which was followed by a number of books and articles written in English on his deeds, which until then had been largely depicted in Hungarian and Swedish.

Wallenberg was born over a century ago on 4 August 1912, the son of one of Sweden's most prominent Protestant families, and was paternally orphaned at birth by the death of his father. He received a cosmopolitan upbringing, travelling widely at a young age and speaking several languages. He studied architecture in Michigan, where he graduated in 1935 with honours. After working in South Africa he spent time in what was then a part of Palestine, where he was trained as a banker hoping to follow in the family business, but he was soon disillusioned with this occupation, and became a director of a food import-export company whose senior partner was a Hungarian Jew. He came into contact with the Jewish tragedy in the wake of Hitler's expulsion of the German Jews. Sensing the misery of the impending Holocaust, Raoul became aware of the inevitability of a brutal catastrophe in Europe.

Diocesi di Acerra
Museo Diocesano

S. E. Mons. Gennaro Verolino
Giusto tra le Nazioni

Giornata della
memoria 2008

Above and right: Memorial book for Gennaro Verolino Righteous Gentile with inscription and photo

Catalogo a cura di
GENNARO NIOLA
ANTONIO PINTAURO
GAETANO CRISPO

Keith Henderson
Tel. (03) 9347 4447

107 Royal Parade
Parkville
Victoria
3052

3/9/01

Dear Frank,

What a master stroke, blending the Star of David and the Cross — and then the inscription — De profundis, Psalm 129, that wonderful prayer for the dead so dear to both Jews & Christians. The original has been a little modified:

De profundis clamavi ad te Domine . Out of the depths I have cried to thee O Lord

Domine, exaudi vocem meam . O Lord hear my voice

and later,

A custodia matutina usque ad . From the morning watch
noctem, speret Israel in   even unto night, let
Domino   Israel hope in the Lord

Warm regards

Keith

Letter from world-renowned neurosurgeon J. Keith Henderson

Wallenberg Plaque by Imre Varga

Original photograph of Raoul Wallenberg (by T. Veres) with personal inscription from his sister Mrs Nina Lagergren

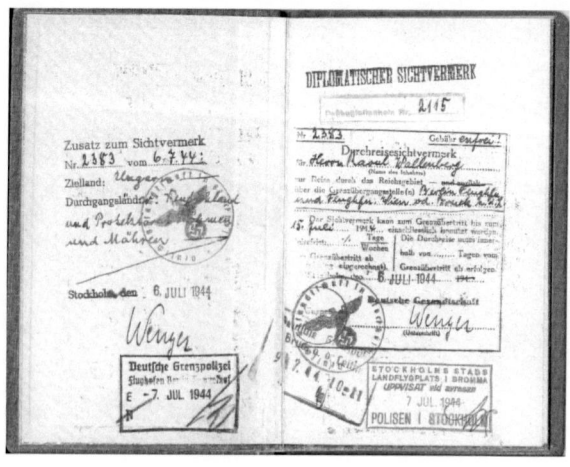

Raoul Wallenberg's diplomatic passport cover and two entries

Graduation, MBBS, 1960

Wedding, Stockholm Town Hall, 1992: Nina Lagergren, Per Anger, Michele Vajda, Frank Vajda, the Mayor of Stockholm, Carl Cederschiöld, Sonja Sonnenfeld, and Simon Raoul in front

Royal Swedish Order of the Polar Star, 2002: A. Hitchcock, J. Graham, F. Vajda, W. Burton, K. McLean, and staff of the Wallenberg Centre of Neuropharmacology in the background

Frank Vajda and His Excellency Ambassador Per Anger, 1983

Mr Jan Anger

Mrs Sonja Sonnenfeld, Secretary of Wallenberg Föreningen, 1983

Mrs Nina Lagergren, Raoul Wallenberg's sister, Simon Raoul and Michele

Michele, John Copland, Sonja Sonnenfeld and Aila Copland

The Grosz family in Paris: Marie Claude (centre), Georges, Pierre, Francois Helen and Antoine, with spouses and children c. 1990

Above: Simon Wiesenthal, Vienna, 1985

Left: Jacob Rosenberg, inspirational writer, poet and friend

Sir Zelman Cowen, former Governor General of Australia,
at Commemoration of Shoah in Hungary, 1944–1994, Melbourne

Frank Vajda, Sir Zelman Cowen and Lady Anna Cowen

Commemoration at the Melbourne Holocaust Museum, 1994

Lifelong friends P. Barta, G. Goldstein, P. de Gail, W. Louis, H. Glasbeek, G. Carr, J. Wilder, P. Farago, R. Lyons. Absent: B. Wilder, M. de Gail, 1963.

Dan McLaughlin, President of the Epilepsy Society of Australia, and Professor Torbjorn Tomson, of the Karolinska Hospital, Stockholm, 2015

Professor P. F. Bladin AO, the "Father of Epilepsy" in Australia and Founder of the Epilepsy and Stroke Societies

Cecilie and Mervyn Lander of Brisbane

Professor Mervyn Eadie AO, leader of Australian clinical neuropharmacology, mentor, co-worker and inspirational friend

G. A. Donnan AO,
Director of the Florey Institute

Collegeaues Dr Mark Newton and John Merory

Professor Mario de Luise

International collaborative group, organised by Piero Perucca, Istanbul 2015: F. Andermann, E. Perucca, S. Berkovic, F. Andermann, T. O'Brien, E. Andermann, L. Laage, D. Battino, T. Tomson, P. Perucca, P. Kwan and F. Vajda

Professor James Best

Professor Athanasios Covanis, President of the International Bureau of Epilepsy, and Professor Emilio Perucca, President of the League Against Epilepsy, awarding the title of Ambassador for Epilepsy to Frank Vajda

Professor Ed Byrne AC DSC, VC of Monash University, Sam Berkovic AC FRS, Fred Mendelsohn AO and Frank Vajda

Professors E. Somerville, T. J. O'Brien, R. Beran and F. Mendelsohn

Professors E. Perucca, T. J. O.Brien and A. Black, and Stephen Davis, President of the International Stroke Association

Governor General Dame Quentin Bryce, Prime Minister of Australia Julia Gillard, Mr Peter Wertheimer and Leader of the Opposition Tony Abbott with the Honorary Citizenship Certificate for Raoul Wallenberg

With Wallenberg's Honorary Australian Citizenship certificate

With son Simon Raoul Leslie, Festschrift, 2015

The late Senator Don Chipp at
Wallenberg Park, 1983

Israel's Ambassador Yssakar Ben Yaacov
unveils the statue, 1985
(sculptor K. Duldig, 1984)

Statue inscription at Wallenberg Park

Saved to Remember: Frank Vajda at Wallenberg Park in Kew, Melbourne

He travelled in Central Europe from 1938 onwards and saw first-hand what Nazism meant, being haunted by the spectre of persecution in Europe. His negotiating skills were shaped by his business experience, but his humanity was present from childhood, and he displayed a compassionate and caring character throughout his life. The wholesale, clockwork-like destruction of the civilian Jewish population in Hungary began after the German occupation on 19 March 1944. The Allies, aware of the magnitude of this horror, appealed to the Regent of Hungary to halt the mass murder, with the newly created War Refugee Board appealing to the world and to neutral countries to send emissaries to help prevent the impending genocide there.

After the occupation of Hungary in 1944 the US War Refugee Board (WRB) was set up to save at least a remnant of the last large Jewish population in Europe. The WRB requested neutral nations to send observers to Hungary to cajole the Hungarians into ceasing to carry out the Final Solution as intended by the Nazis. Sweden agreed to help in this way, initially the only country to do so. Wallenberg volunteered, and was approved by Sweden's Foreign Office and blessed by the rabbi of Stockholm. He was advised about conditions in Hungary by a number of experts, and financed by the WRB, the American Joint Distribution Committee and the Swedish Government. He was specifically sent to save Jews. He requested diplomatic status, adequate finance, freedom to approach any group in Hungary, and freedom from the restraint of conventional diplomatic channels. He knew his mission was difficult and dangerous, requiring negotiation, bribery, and the use of pressure. Wallenberg was determined to succeed in a situation where before him there had been only tears, failure, brutality and murder.

In Hungary

Wallenberg was accredited as a secretary to the Swedish Embassy in Hungary. Jews from the provinces have been deported, so he concentrated his efforts on Budapest. He arrived on 9 July 1944, just too late see the last train from the outer Budapest suburbs leaving for Auschwitz three days earlier. From then until 17 January 1945, this man organised, with the help of his Swedish colleagues and other neutral diplomats, a rescue network which resulted in stalling the Nazi war machine, eventually saving many thousands of Jews doomed to destruction. Wallenberg was assisted by a staff of hundreds in the Swedish Embassy, located in several office buildings. He supported similar activities by the representatives of other neutral countries, as well as collaborating with the Red Cross and with underground Jewish rescue organisations.

Wallenberg contacted the *Judenrat* (the Jewish Council), opposition personalities, influential non-Jews, resistance and other groups. He provided apartment buildings to house those he was sheltering in a so-called International Ghetto, which was supplied with food, medicines, and a degree of protection provided by the Swedish Embassy. The hospital our family lived in was a Wallenberg creation. In these endeavours Wallenberg catered for Hungarian as well as Jewish civilians, and even on occasion for Arrow Cross militia who accepted his offers of help. Wallenberg alternatively threatened, rewarded and resisted Nazi officials. By bribing primitive, poverty-stricken vigilantes he was able to rescue many intended victims from the grasp of their captors. He prevented slave labour battalions from being deported, had Jews released from internment, and in general helped to stabilise the status of the 200,000 Jewish inhabitants of the city.

Wallenberg also acted in his formal diplomatic capacity, constantly bombarding the authorities with appeals, diplomatic notes and memoranda, which set out details of the brutal behaviour of the militia, which he claimed was incompatible with Sweden's formal recognition of the Hungarian Government. He promised better relations if the Hungarian attitude towards his Swedish citizen protégés, who were in effect the Jewish population, improved. On a personal level, Wallenberg attended the death marches, providing food and blankets to a desperately tired and moribund people on the way to extinction. An official diplomat to join him in this activity was his fellow Swede Per Anger, later widely honoured for his deeds. Wallenberg removed people from deportation trains, rescued children out of convoys and returned groups of people close to the German border before they could be transferred to Eichmann's hands. When alerted, he rushed to execution sites, often at night, on the banks of the Danube river, saving hundreds of people in the face of power-crazy murderers by using his assumed power, his charisma and bribes to induce the release of his 'Swedish protégés'. I owe my life to this.

Eichmann planned for the deportation of Budapest Jews in August 1944. Protests by the King of Sweden, Gustav V, the Pope, Sir Anthony Eden and others forced Admiral Horthy to stop this action. In addition Horthy used his remaining power to sack Nazi fanatics in the ministry, which temporarily improved the situation. But the resurgence of the Hungarian fascists, the Arrow Cross, in October 1944, threatened once more the existence of all the remaining Jews trapped in Budapest. Eichmann returned and deportations on foot began. At this juncture Wallenberg took over as the principal diplomatic presence in Budapest, totally concerned with slowing down the bloodbath. He persuaded the new Arrow Cross Foreign Minister to continue to recognise his *Schutzpasses*, a major triumph – 20,000 were issued. In the last three months of the war Wallenberg embarked on a series of individual rescue attempts. As the danger grew, so did his level of activity. He took people from the sealed ghetto and removed them to the protected ghetto, where conditions were less horrible. He had numerous Hungarian, Jewish and diplomatic supporters in these endeavours.

Eichmann departed Budapest during the siege by the Red Army; before he left he issued orders to raze the ghetto and machine gun its inhabitants. This order began to be set in motion, with the names of the execution squads known and ready to go into action. Wallenberg saved the ghetto by sending a message to the commanding SS General, charging him with criminal responsibility if he carried out the order and threatening to testify against him after the war. The Nazi cancelled the action. This act alone saved 80,000 Jews. A book on these events, published in 1948 in Hungary by Jenõ Lévai, describes quite clearly the details of this planned mass murder, naming the principal German and Hungarian units involved and their criminal commanders, who were to embark on the machine gunning of the inhabitants within a few hours. This book documents that virtually all Jews who survived in Budapest owe their lives to Wallenberg. This contrasts with the situation in provincial Hungary and in other countries, where only a tiny fraction of Jews were able to escape.

The Soviets Arrive

At the time of the arrival of the Red Army and the Liberation of Budapest in early 1945, Wallenberg reported to the occupying Soviet forces in order to meet the Soviet General Rodion Malinovsky, and to ask for help in rebuilding the lives of the Budapest population. He was taken into 'protective custody' by Soviet military intelligence, known as SMERSH, with the involvement of General Serov, later Nikita Khrushchev's henchman, and imprisoned in the Lubyanka prison in Moscow. Over twenty people have subsequently testified to having seen him in a variety of Soviet prisons. Having succeeded in foiling the plans of one Fascist system, Wallenberg was kidnapped and kept in prison by a second group of totalitarian criminals. His arrest and the Russians' failure to release him is one of the greatest personal tragedies of World War Two. The debate about what happened to him continues.

The Swedish Wallenberg Association and the Swedish Government have plenty of evidence to back up the view that the Soviets were lying, and that the

KGB continued to cover up evidence of Wallenberg's whereabouts. He may have been alive for decades after his arrest and kept in a silent camp, together with other survivors of Soviet war crimes; there are even suggestions he may have been kept in a psychiatric prison. There was systematic obstruction and evasion by the KGB and its successors, which continues to be a state within the state, even after the collapse of Communism.

In the end Raoul Wallenberg gave his life for the people whom he saved. This does not mean he died in doing so, but life in a Soviet prison meant sacrificing his own life. Someone who knew him well has said of him:

> In the darkest days, Raoul needed an additional sixty office workers to manufacture his documents and help distribute food and work in administration. He gave the order to employ them. Someone asked: 'Jews or non-Jews?' Raoul got angry: 'I said employ sixty people. I do not recognise a difference.'

In 1944 in Budapest he must have been a rare person able to make that statement. To me this says everything about this Hero of the Holocaust.

From an early age I was fully aware of Wallenberg's role in trying to help us in the period of genocide. What I have learnt since has only confirmed my earlier impressions. People even now, decades later, have tears in their eyes when they tell of their personal encounters with him. From time to time I was asked what it would mean to me if Raoul Wallenberg were to return from captivity in the Soviet Union. I replied it would mean as much as if my father returned from the martyrdom of a concentration camp.

It was said by the head of the Jewish community in Budapest after the war that one of the greatest achievements of Wallenberg had been to restore the feeling of humanity in the Jews of Budapest, giving them hope of not being totally abandoned by the world in their hour of despair. This thirty-two year old Swedish diplomat was acting as the eyes and ears of the world at a time when the world under the German yoke had descended to barbaric mass murder. The killers could not operate unhindered; every move they made was observed and reported by this man, who can justly be regarded as one of the most important figures to emerge from the conflict.

Simon Wiesenthal

I first heard about Simon Wiesenthal in 1960 when a news article about the capture of Eichmann attracted my attention. Wiesenthal has been described as the world's foremost Nazi hunter, and he gained my avid support. At least here was one man who had not forgotten, and what is more he had acted on what he remembered and been successful. Wiesenthal did not try to assassinate Nazi criminals, which is what I would have liked to do, but acted within the law, which caused him tremendous frustration, but he never abandoned this moral stance.

Born in Galicia in 1908, Wiesenthal became an architect, was imprisoned in concentration camps by the Nazis in Poland, and eventually liberated from the Mauthausen camp. He set up an international organisation, the Jewish Documentation Centre, which systematically collected data on Nazi war criminals, and has brought more than a thousand of them to justice. In 1979, when a forum was set up in Stockholm to try to locate and free Raoul Wallenberg, Wiesenthal contributed to that campaign as much any other individual. We struck up a friendship in 1982, which lasted for the remaining twenty-two years of his life. The book my cousin Elizabeth Pudler bought for me, written by Wiesenthal, remains in my collection of autographed books, signed by this great man who remembered what happened in history.

I first met Wiesenthal in his small office located in the old Jewish quarter of Vienna; because of attempts on his life by neo-Nazi thugs, the Austrian government provided a permanent armed police guard, who sat in the corridor outside his office to forestall further attempts on his life. His office staff consisted of one or two devoted secretaries, and his rooms were overflowing with books and documents. We spoke of Wallenberg, for whom he felt more should have been done by Sweden after the war, blaming the Swedish government's fear of Russia for this neglect. He then spoke about Mauthausen, one of the camps he had been imprisoned in during the Holocaust. We spoke about Ebensee, and of my mother's early attempts to locate her husband's grave. In his opinion, my father was probably cremated; Wiesenthal's view is in accord with the record of the Stadtsamt Gemeinde Mauthausen, as we have seen earlier.

Wiesenthal spoke of his determination to continue to track down the murderers, and made a request to me:

> Try to set up a committee to protest neo-Nazi outrages and get other people involved. It was not only the Jews who were the objects of Nazi hatred. The Slavs, Dutch, gypsies and many others were also targeted. If a body of former Nazi victims were to speak out against graffiti, swastika-daubing, and inflammatory revisionism, it would be more effective as a protest.

I gave him a list of many people who would financially support his endeavours. We parted good friends.

Wiesenthal and I remained in contact for the next twenty years. When my son was born, as noted, I proudly named him Simon. Each year we exchanged letters and we met on four more occasions, including once at his home – he was in his late eighties at the time. He gave me ten of his books, published in five languages, inscribed with good wishes. On one occasion I was very proud to have been mentioned in his annual *Newsletter* in relation to Raoul Wallenberg, our common focus of endeavour. I endowed a scholarship at my old school in his honour, and attend the school annual speech nights where the Wiesenthal Prize for Community Service is awarded. I undertook a mission for him when he was looking for an escaped Nazi war criminal, but sadly could not locate him. I supported his Documentation Centre in Vienna, which was funded by private donations, mainly by Dutch survivors.

Wiesenthal spent most of his life pursuing war criminals with spectacular success, and he said that he did so in order that when he met his Maker, and his departed brethren, he could look them in the eye and say: 'I have not forgotten you'. He has had his detractors over the years, but his achievements speak louder than words. He remains supreme in my estimation as a symbol of justice, being the most remarkable man I have ever met.

Per Anger

In 1982, after my enthusiasm in trying to liberate Wallenberg had been kindled, I wrote to the Raoul Wallenberg Forum in Stockholm, and received a very courteous answer from Nina Lagergeren. This spurred me on. I called on the Swedish Consulate here, which gave me a book by Ambassador Per Anger, who had served in Australia in the seventies, and who had been a colleague and fellow rescuer with Raoul Wallenberg in Budapest in 1944–45. Soon after I heard from Sonja Sonnenfeld that His Excellency Ambassador Anger was arriving on a boat for a visit to Australia. During his visit we spent almost a whole day talking, punctuated by lunch.

Subsequently I have had the opportunity of meeting him on numerous occasions, I have been his guest in Sweden, and have appeared with him at public gatherings. We arranged a function called 'Tribute to Wallenberg' at the University of Melbourne where Per Anger spoke together with a number of dignitaries including Federal and State Parliamentarians. He addressed the B'nai B'rith Wallenberg Unit and spoke at the Melbourne Holocaust

Museum. In Sydney he gave a talk to a meeting of the local Wallenberg Committee. I was able to collaborate with him in anticipation of an address he was invited to deliver at San Remo in Italy for a Noble Peace Prize gathering.

At the time of Gorbachev's accession as head of the USSR, we appeared together with Mrs Lagergeren on US television to plead for Raoul Wallenberg's release. Per Anger participated in a US Congress hearing in 1983, during which I also gave testimony. Ambassador Anger was a principal figure at the 'Tribute to Wallenberg' in New York in 1985, with the participation of Isaac Stern and major public figures at Carnegie Hall. He joined the invitees at the launch of the film *Wallenberg: A Hero's Story*, in New York, where I asked the film star Richard Chamberlain, who played Wallenberg in the film, to lend support to the cause. Anger introduced this dramatic film which has a segment depicting his own role. His book, *With Raoul Wallenberg in Budapest: Memories of the War Years in Hungary*, has been translated into Hungarian.

Per Anger regularly discussed his activities with me and answered questions about the Swedish rescue mission, to which no other person could authoritatively respond to. Ambassador Anger became the President of the Raoul Wallenberg Association in Sweden, and did as much as Simon Wiesenthal in trying to uncover Wallenberg's fate. He worked in close association with Sonja Sonnenfeld, who acted as secretary to the Association for three decades. Ambassador Anger has been awarded Israel's highest decoration 'Righteous Gentile', has had a tree planted in his honour at the *Allée des Justes* in Jerusalem, and subsequently has been made an Honorary Citizen of Israel.

On Anger's seventy-fifth birthday, I had the singular honour of being asked to speak in Stockholm on his important role in saving lives in wartime Budapest. The birthday function was a glittering affair. In addressing this gathering I mentioned that he has been a diplomatic representative for Sweden for some years before the German takeover, and that he was the first man to whom the threatened Jewish community turned for advice and help. Anger used his knowledge of the Nansen passports of World War One, a symbolic document offering protection for people with Swedish connections. He devised a Provisional Passport, the so-called *Bescheinigung*. These provisional documents, issued in small numbers, actually allowed some Jewish people to be exempted from the requirement to wear the yellow star, and permitted them to move about in spite of the curfew restricting the movement of Jews. This enabled them to seek further help, and make plans to escape the restrictions and threat of deportation. These passports were tested in court and were accepted by the Hungarian authorities.

The *Schutzpass* Wallenberg deployed was in Swedish colours; it included a photograph, was bilingual and was more difficult to forge than the others. There existed other forms of documentation issued by the neutral nations. The Swiss *Schutzbrief*, for example, was a sheet of white paper with a typed standard text, into which the name of the holder and his family could be inserted relatively easily. But the Swedish one was held to be the most valuable, gaining the most respect from both the Germans and the Hungarian Arrow Cross. Swedish papers were, in addition, signed by the Ambassador Danielsson, who never refused to authenticate the documents, although he knew that in a strict legal sense they were based on fiction.

The second major contribution of the Swedes was the delivery of their King Gustaf V's telegram to the Regent Horthy. This has since been regarded as a crucial factor in the cancellation of the deportation from the capital. In this action Anger represented the Ambassador, who for some reason was not available. Anger was I believe the only professional diplomat to assist Wallenberg in going to the aid of helpless civilians on the way to extinction. There were other volunteers, civilians, officials friendly to Wallenberg, and some priests, but only one other diplomat, Per Anger.

I mentioned in my talk Anger's role after the war in fighting for his friend in the Swedish Foreign Office, trying to combat the hesitation which prevailed when the Swedish government readily accepted the word of Stalin's henchmen that Wallenberg was not in Soviet hands. Exchanges of information were spurned and US help, which had been offered, was also declined. Per Anger did not take kindly to this and resigned from the Wallenberg desk. His future career as a diplomat brought a great deal of credit to him and his country. He campaigned fearlessly for Wallenberg and advocated a strong line against the Soviets, claiming that they only respect strength. But it was not meant to be.

In 2002 after a brief illness Per Anger passed away. I was asked to speak on behalf of those he had saved and the funeral, held in Stockholm, had the proportions of a State event. Per has been honoured widely, and after his passing Sweden instituted a Per Anger Prize for humanitarian deeds, awarded annually to worthy candidates worldwide. The inaugural recipient was his close friend, Archbishop Verolino, with whom he had worked in close collaboration in Hungary in 1944, and whose contribution will be described later in this book. Per Anger was a great man, and a loyal friend. All those who knew him were enriched by his presence.

Chapter Twelve

THE SOVIET CONNECTION

Witnesses

What happened to Wallenberg? In 1945 after his disappearance the Soviet Union announced that he was in 'protective custody'. They later changed the story and stated that he had never been seen in the Soviet Union. They persisted with this story in spite of Swedish interventions until, due to the overwhelming volume of evidence, the Soviet Foreign Minister Gromyko in 1957 admitted that Wallenberg had indeed been arrested by the secret police and had been in the Lubyanka prison, but Gromyko said, he had he died in 1947 from a heart attack. The only evidence produced was a medical officer's note to the head of State Security, Abakumov, claiming that the prisoner died of a heart attack and was cremated.

This document has been sceptically received and is widely regarded to be a forgery, based as it was on a number of dubious claims: that Wallenberg was cremated, which was not a common practice, that he died at thirty-three from a heart attack, and that a doctor wrote directly to the Security Chief directly, which was a breach of protocol. There was an absence of other documents relating to the case, and most importantly a number of reputable witnesses of many nationalities had seen Wallenberg after 1947. The Soviet media and their Hungarian vassals always maintained that all people who said Wallenberg was alive were motivated by greed, wishing to extort money from his wealthy Swedish relatives. Nothing could be further from the truth. Witnesses who over decades claimed to have seen Wallenberg in a variety of Soviet prisons had nothing to gain by giving this information, except the wrath and attention of the KGB, who looked very unfavourably upon anyone speaking on this subject. One of my relatives, who met Wallenberg after his own mother was taken, was unwilling to take an Israeli stamp of Wallenberg to Hungary, because his wife was afraid of being searched on the Hungarian-Austrian border, not daring to risk having a taboo object, Wallenberg's picture, in their possession.

The official Soviet line between 1957 and the 1985 arrival of Gorbachev was that anyone claiming Wallenberg was alive was fanning hostile propaganda against the Soviet Union. It is against this background that the accuracy and bravery of the witnesses speaking out about him must be judged. Only a few sightings will be mentioned here. All those Swiss, Italian, Austrian and German prisoners of war, who on their release supplied information about Raoul Wallenberg in Soviet prisons, stated that Raoul gave them the same message to pass on: 'Go to the nearest Swedish Embassy and say that you have met Raoul Wallenberg, who saved Jews in Hungary during the war. They will know what to do'. But alas Wallenberg was wrong, the Swedes never did know what to do, nor dare do it. But under the weight of this evidence, presented over a twelve year period between Wallenberg's arrest and 1957, the Soviets were forced to admit that they had been lying. Thus these 'hostile propagandists' were in fact honest witnesses.

Professor Marvin Makinen from Chicago was a prisoner in the USSR after his arrest as an alleged spy in 1959. He knew of a Swedish prisoner, kept in a solitary cell, whose name was Vandenberg, and who saved many Jews during the war. He spoke to prisoners who have seen this prisoner frequently, and they spoke of him in the prison amongst themselves. Makinen was exchanged in 1961. He reported about the Swede to the Swedish Embassy in the US after his release. The Swedes told him it was their responsibility for any further action, and to forget about the prisoner. He did so until 1979, when the explosion of interest about Wallenberg suddenly enlightened him about the 'Swedish prisoner Vandenberg'. He went to Sweden and met the Wallenberg Association, which found that the Swedish Government had done nothing with the information supplied twenty years earlier. I have met Makinen in the US and I am convinced of his honesty. His name will crop up again.

A Russian Jew called Kalinski claimed in 1978 to have seen Wallenberg for years in the Vladimir prison in the 1950s and 60s. He even wrote about him to his sister is Israel, referring to him as the Swede who saved Jews in Rumania during the war. I have seen the postcards by Kalinski. He claimed he referred to Rumania to confuse the KGB. He will also be mentioned again. In the 60s, 70s and 80s, and as recently as 1989, there have been many such sightings of Wallenberg. Simultaneously there have been articles in the Soviet and Hungarian press, as well as in the Swedish media, with various accounts of Wallenberg's death. But as Wallenberg's family has stated: 'You can only die once, but you can be seen in many places, if you are shifted from prison to prison.'

A Protest to the Soviet Embassy

In 1982 a committee aiming to introduce the world to the plight of Raoul Wallenberg was initiated by the Australasian Union of Jewish Students (AUJS). Led by Karen Schiff and Danny Ungar, a petition, directed at the USSR and protesting against Wallenberg's detention, was drawn up and publicised in the newspapers. The collection of signatures began at a rally, where petition sheets were distributed. About 3000 signatures were collected. But it soon became clear that the legacy of fear induced by the KGB intimidated many potential signatories. The people most interested in supporting the Wallenberg cause were not necessarily Jewish. The majority of people subsequently involved were those with humanitarian aspirations and a sense of justice, coupled with admiration for a hero.

An interested person suggested the Committee involve a high level political figure to kindle interest in the Wallenberg case, and so obtain Parliamentary support for its activities. We arranged to convene a three man Parliamentary delegation to deliver the protest signatures to the Soviet Embassy. The Democrat Senator Don Chipp was enthusiastic; for many years subsequently he functioned as the main parliamentary supporter on behalf of the Wallenberg Committee. In addition Mr Peter Falconer, a Liberal MP, supported by the Labor Senator John Button, joined me in delivering the petition. I was the one nominated to hand it over, but we were warned earlier by the USSR spokesman that while they would accept the petition, no speeches or discussions were permitted.

On arrival at the Soviet Embassy we were admitted to a hallway. I handed over the book of signatures, protesting the injustice perpetrated against the Swedish diplomat, a citizen of a neutral country in 1945, as indeed it still was in 1982. A secretary of the Soviet Embassy said: 'What am I to do with this book?' I replied by making a speech, contrary to our agreement. I spoke of Wallenberg's heroism, his activities to save lives threatened by the common Fascist enemy. Finally I raised the question of a gross infringement of justice, and of the laws of humanity, in keeping him incarcerated. The spokesman replied: 'We know nothing of this man.' I suggested that it was their duty to find out where he was located, and to free him.

The Russians did not reply, and the meeting was over, with no commitment obtained. We then left the building, after which I said something which indicates my incredible naivety. I recall saying to Danny Ungar, who was a law student at the time: 'The Russian seemed a pleasant enough man.' Ungar replied: 'A KGB man, a thug like all others in such a position. They are KGB men and we can be certain of having been filmed and recorded.'

After our return from Canberra we discussed the Soviet response, realising that the Russians were not even following their own party line. Their Foreign Minister Gromyko had stated in 1957 that Wallenberg had died of a heart attack at the age of thirty-three, on 17 July 1947. We wrote to the USSR Embassy immediately, pointing out their own inconsistency. The reply took six weeks. The Soviet Embassy called us on the telephone: 'We apologise for not being fully informed on this matter. You were right about Gromyko's report. Wallenberg has died, and anyone using this issue to protest against the Soviet Union is only fanning the flames of anti-Soviet propaganda.' This was a foretaste of many similar comments in the future. Senator Chipp made a speech in Parliament about Wallenberg at this time. His support was always valuable and deeply appreciated.

The Gorbachev Period

When in 1985 Gorbachev came to power a reassessment of the case was expected. People asked 'What is the purpose of keeping Wallenberg in jail, when Gorbachev could claim goodwill from his release?' The tragic thing was that Wallenberg was not a priority for Gorbachev, who had received sufficient plaudits already, including the Nobel Peace Prize, and he had no absolute control over the KGB. Gorbachev knew about Wallenberg, as he was told personally by members close to the Wallenberg family about their belief that he was a prisoner alive in the Gulag. The German Chancellor Kohl believed when he was in office that Wallenberg was still alive. In a letter written to many Wallenberg support groups he referred to Wallenberg as the most influential hero of the century and acknowledged German responsibility for his arrest. Kohl pressed Gorbachev repeatedly to reveal the truth about Wallenberg, and to let him go if he was alive.

In 1989 Wallenberg's brother and sister and closest supporters, including Ambassador Per Anger and Mrs Sonnenfeld, secretary of the Raoul Wallenberg Association, went to Moscow at the invitation of the Soviet authorities. They were given Wallenberg's notebooks, some of his money, passport and prison registration cards, which were miraculously turned up by the KGB the week before the visit. This after claiming to have no documents pertaining to Wallenberg for forty-five years. In November 1989 the Soviets accepted the fact that no evidence existed that Wallenberg died in 1947. There has been increasing interest in Wallenberg in the Soviet media and two films, one by the Swedes and one by the Russians, spread knowledge about him in the USSR. But the KGB was still a state within the state, and the truth was hushed up.

In 1990 the Soviet Government, under the weight of continuous petitions and press publicity, allowed a team of Western experts, led by the former dissidents Professor Makinen and Guy von Dardel, Wallenberg's brother, to enter Russia to conduct the first investigation ever to take place into Wallenberg's disappearance. They were allowed to film all the prisoner cards they wished. Several hundred prisoners' cards from the Vladimir prison were videotaped and analysed in Sweden. Raoul's file was not turned up, obviously removed and held by the KGB. But the cards of a number of witnesses were found.

Analysis of the other prisoners' documents indicated that those who gave evidence about meeting Raoul in the Gulag had told the truth about every detail of their past, their transit dates and their imprisonment. In particular it was shown that Kalinski was also truthful about his transfers from prison to prison in the company of Wallenberg. This and other testimonies indicate that Wallenberg certainly did not die in 1947, and that he was alive in the 1970s and 80s. But his passing is shrouded in evasion.

A Russian Journalist's Investigations

Alexei Karcev, a reporter on *Komsomolskaya Pravda*, a relatively liberal Soviet journal, who was investigating the fate of Raoul Wallenberg, wrote a letter to Vladimir Krushchov, head of the KGB, in 1990. On the basis of the reply received from the KGB and on the basis of information not from official sources, more facts have emerged about people who had met Wallenberg in Soviet captivity. Karcev wrote:

> About two months after I wrote to Vladimir Krushchov the telephone rang and associates from the KGB invited me to a meeting. They promised to answer in part questions I put to their boss Krushchov, head of the KGB. We met the next day in a room in a small street close to the Ljubjanka, where according to many witnesses Wallenberg was kept imprisoned from 1945 to 1947.

Two officers in civilian clothes met the journalist in the spirit of the new glasnost. They read the answers to his questions, and showed him a report about Wallenberg's death in 1947, signed by Col. Smoltsov, medical chief of the Ljubjanka prison. Smoltsov's handwritten report had also been shown to Wallenberg's relatives and friends in October 1989. The KGB denied requests asking the name of the unit responsible for his arrest. Was there something to hide? The mysterious year of 1947 was also a fateful one for Dr Smoltsov. That year he was pensioned off because of serious heart disease and over the next six years he virtually never left his home before dying of heart failure, after which he was buried in the Vagankovsk cemetery.

In order to check Smoltsov's report about the death of the Swedish diplomat, Karcev asked the KGB to name other doctors who worked at the Ljubjanka prison hospital at the same time as Smoltsov. This request was refused, as the KGB maintained that in their archives it was impossible to identify any of Smoltsov's former colleagues. The KGB also refused to name those guards who between 1945 and 1947 had worked in the Ljubjanka and Lefortovo prisons and so could have been expected to have known Wallenberg. The KGB claimed not to have kept 'lists of these people'. *Komsomolskaya Pravda* has found out the names of five NKVD (Internal Security) investigators who according to testimonies interrogated Wallenberg in the Ljubjanka.

Other questions left unanswered were the names of leaders of SMERSH, the Soviet military counterintelligence body, in 1945. The name of the organisation is an acronym for 'Death to Spies' (Смерть шпионам). Karcev was able to discover that SMERSH had been responsible for the arrest of the diplomat Wallenberg. Representatives of State Security declined to name the heads of SMERSH in spite of the fact that the story Karcev was investigating took place more than forty years ago. Using independent sources and witnesses Karcev was able to ascertain that one of the heads of Soviet military counterintelligence was Ivan Alex Serov, later Minister for State Security. There is another man, on account of whose later position the Soviets would not recognise Wallenberg's arrest for half a century, and who now claims to have no documents whatever in connection with this matter. This man, General Ivashutin, was the commander of military counterintelligence for the Third Ukrainian Front of the Red Army which liberated Budapest.

Seven Decades On

Even in Russia under Vladimir Putin there are monuments, research institutes, articles, and associations of people formed to honour and commemorate Wallenberg. Thus it appears the current political climate in Russia seems to favour solving the mystery as to what really happened to Wallenberg. President Putin could claim credit for a positive move in an unresolved war crime committed by his predecessors, just as he has done over the Katyn massacre by the Soviets in Poland.

It is inconceivable that the truth be permanently hidden. Historically the USSR was one of the world's most bureaucratic regimes. Matters of state were always meticulously documented. Several copies of what took place in the Wallenberg case are reported to be filed in numerous archives, possibly including the archives of the president, the party, SMERSH, the Ministry of the Interior, and the prisons' and prosecutor's office, as well as numerous state and district libraries. Some of these could be hiding the truth, and it is within the power of Russia's leaders to reveal it.

I do not think Wallenberg's fate can be clarified by physical force, bribery or secret activity against any agency or state. It can only be attempted by applying the force of 'public opinion' in the widest sense. Putin does not need to have the benefits of openness pointed out to him. A letter to Putin may be accompanied by a personal letter from major Western leaders, but the main thrust is the widespread action of international figures representing a concerted, non-political move. In this vein I wrote the following letter to President Putin in 2014 to ask for the truth.

President Vladimir Putin
President of Russia
Office of the President
Kremlin
Moscow
Russia

Your Excellency, Mr. Putin,

At this time of international turmoil I am reminded of 1945 when I was liberated by troops of the glorious Red Army in Budapest, and I was allowed to lead a productive life for the last 70 years.

I was saved from the firing squad by the Swedish businessman Raoul Wallenberg, but the liberation from the fascists of Hungary and Germany was only possible by the victory of Russia over the fascists.

Meantime I learnt that Wallenberg was in Soviet hands and may have been the victim of Stalinist terror, which your regime condemns.

Wallenberg's fate is important to me and to many of those who gained benefit from his activities, for which he was later wrongly apprehended.

Recently I was able to influence Australia to make Wallenberg an honorary citizen, 70 years after the war and his arrest.

I now appeal to you Mr. President to order your officials to release the data on what has actually happened to this man. The amount of sympathy this would generate for you world wide is inestimable, millions would applaud your action. Please consider.

Please accept my most profound expressions of respect.

Yours sincerely,

Professor Frank Vajda AM

Another initiative was to write a note to the Lord Mayor of Budapest, a man who admires Wallenberg deeply, and displays a photo of the Swedish rescuer on his desk.

Lord Mayor of Budapest
Town Hall Budapest
Hungary

Dear Mr Demszky,

I have the honour of writing to you at the suggestion of Mrs. Nina Lagergren, Raoul Wallenberg's sister, in Sweden

We ask you most respectfully, to make contact with members of the Hungarian delegates to the European parliament in Strasbourg, and ask them to support a proposal requesting President Vladimir Putin, to release the archives which reveal the fate suffered by Raoul Wallenberg at the hands of the Soviet authorities, since his kidnapping in 1945.

It is almost certain that documentary evidence exists, but it has never been released and it covers up crimes which are not the fault to the current regime, hence should not be hidden 60 years after the event.

We would be grateful for Hungary to add its voice to those of other European civilised nations in asking Russia to account for the truth. This so far has been consistently denied and the matter never addressed honestly.

Yours humbly,

Nina Lagergren, Raoul Wallenberg's sister

Frank Vajda, saved by Wallenberg

Neither letter received a reply.

Chapter Thirteen

ARCHBISHOP VEROLINO, ONE OF THE RIGHTEOUS

Verolino in Hungary

Raoul Wallenberg's colleague, Swedish Ambassador Per Anger, often referred in conversation to a saintly man, an Italian priest, Monsignor Gennaro Verolino. During the Holocaust in Hungary, this wonderful man saved many lives by a combination of personal courage, resourcefulness and using his status as a Catholic bishop of high standing in a Catholic country.

Monsignor Verolino worked alongside Angelo Rotta, the senior Vatican envoy in Budapest and doyen of the diplomatic corps to the court of the Hungarian Regent, Horthy, during the Nazi occupation. Monsignor Verolino's title, *Uditore*, ranked him as Deputy to the Vatican Delegate, or as Secretary of the Vatican Mission. Disregarding conventional diplomatic protocols, to save Jewish lives, Verolino prepared a 'special paper' for the Head of the Vatican Embassy, calling for immediate intervention with the extreme right-wing government agencies, who were embarked on a program of deportations or mass murder on the spot for those whose racial origin was anathema to them.

Angelo Rotta, a distinguished prelate, who had exerted himself in Slovakia on behalf of the condemned Jewish minority since 1941, succeeded in staving off deportations from that country for many months. Being fully aware of the outcome of deportations he did not shirk from stating that 'the meaning of deportations is death'. Rotta was able to convene a meeting of all the neutral diplomatic representatives in Budapest including Raoul Wallenberg from Sweden, Charles Lutz from Switzerland, Ambassador Sans Bris from Portugal, Georgio Perlasca, who was the Spanish representative, Valdemar Langlet of the Swedish Red Cross, as well as Borman of the International Red Cross.

The conference resulted in a memorandum, sent to the Arrow Cross leader Ferenc Szálasi, the so-called 'Leader of the Nation', protesting in the strongest possible terms against the inhumanity of continued extermination of the Jewish population. The names of the diplomats mentioned above have become revered. In spite of his tremendous efforts in support of the Rotta and the Vatican mission, Verolino was for many decades never recognised nor given any public honour for his wonderful achievements. That was the case until 2005, when Kate Wacz, a tireless investigator of these matters who was herself saved in Budapest in 1944, discovered that the venerable Archbishop was well and living in retirement in Rome. He was immediately visited by this lady from Sweden. The discovery was communicated to the Swedish Government and to the Yad Vashem memorial centre in Israel, the 'Heroes' and Martyrs' Authority', which can bestow the title 'Righteous amongst the Nations', which signifies that those 'who save one life, act as though they had saved the whole world'.

Monsignor Verolino, a frail gentleman aged ninety-nine but in full possession of his faculties, was surprised. He was pleased to meet people who had been saved, but did not wish to get recognition, or be given any honour. 'I did what my conscience told me', he said. This is exactly what the vast majority of the Righteous reply when asked 'Why did you do it?'

Awards to Monsignor Verolino

The Per Anger Award's first recipient, following the wishes of Anger's family and the officials of the Swedish Government, was Monsignor Verolino of Rome. The ceremony was attended by the Swedish Prime Minister Goran Persson, the Vatican Secretary of State, Kate Wacz who had found Verolino in 2005, the family of Ambassador Anger and several hundred international dignitaries. The distinguished Archbishop did not wish to accept the prize, but was prevailed upon to change his mind when it was explained that he could donate the monetary reward to charity immediately afterwards, which is what happened.

Further moves to get him recognised by Israel followed, but did not follow automatically. Yad Vashem's response to requests to honour this man with the title of Righteous Gentile was negative. The fatuous explanation was that Verolino was only Monsignor Rotta's secretary and did what he was told. This was below contempt. A second argument advanced was that he could not receive the title as he had already been sent a 'nice letter'. This compounded the crass stupidity of officialdom. Thirdly there were 'no eyewitnesses'.

As someone proposed for the title stated: 'When I pulled people out of a deportation convoy and hid them, I did not say to them: "I am Mr. X. Y., please remember my name because I may need you to bear eyewitness testimony for an organisation in Israel that will demand that I present documentation for what I had done."

It so happened that the people who had discovered Verolino's address in Rome had also managed to get hold of eyewitnesses, who in the most detailed terms described the heroism of Verolino. He had barred the Nazi terrorists from the Vatican building where he had hidden Jewish children, daring the gangsters to harm him, thus saving about twenty children during this one episode. There were many others. Verolino's name is widely documented in the history of the Holocaust, by Jenő Lévai amongst others, the writer who immortalised the deeds of Wallenberg. In spite of this Yad Vashem stuck to its refusal to grant recognition. At this point, an American activist assembled a detailed document of forty-five pages and sent it to Israel proposing Verolino for the title of the 'Righteous Gentile'. This man asked me to provide him with original documents and when he received them he looked surprised and said: 'But they are not written in English? What am I to do with them?' It was explained to him that documents created at the time were not written in English. Yad Vashem responded simply by asking this well-meaning person 'to make it shorter'. Subtlety is not a hallmark of officialdom.

I wrote a brief letter, pointing out that the Yad Vashem officials were mistaken in believing that Verolino was only a minor official. His title 'Secretary' (*Uditore*) does not mean a typist, or a filing clerk or someone taking dictation. Henry Kissinger was Secretary of State for the United States, Kofi Annan was Secretary General of the United Nations, and Stalin was Secretary of the Soviet Communist Party. Not exactly typists. In addition to this translation error, the officials were grossly negligent in understanding the great service Archbishop Verolino had rendered to the Jewish people at the hour of their greatest peril. It was time they corrected their mistake. I signed my letter on a letterhead to make it look official, having learnt that real or imaginary titles and position appear more important to second-rate bureaucrats than the real values of humanity and compassion. The Nazis respected the *Schutzpass* because of the stamps, photos and signatures it bore.

When I returned to Sweden the following year I was shown the reply from Yad Vashem, granting Monsignor Verolino the title of 'One of the Righteous in the World'. Sadly he had died about six months earlier.

The Vatican Conference on the Holocaust

In May 2012 I received an invitation sent by the Swedish Ambassador to the Vatican to attend a proposed meeting in Rome. The Swedish Foreign Office, in association with the Vatican, wished to hold a seminar about the rescue of Jews in Hungary, involving not only Sweden but the neutral diplomats and other humanitarians who assisted and supported Wallenberg. The seminar was given the title 'Coraggio contra il Male' (Courage in the Face of Evil). The title of the seminar was later extended to specifically mention Wallenberg, Anger, Verolino and the aftermath of the Liberation. A particular interest of the Vatican was in the role played by Per Anger's close friend, Msgr. Gennaro Verolino, who saved many lives, especially children, from the Arrow Cross and who disappeared after the war. Rome wished me to speak about him in the context of the situation in Budapest in 1944.

It was planned to involve the community of Sant'Egidio, a benevolent community group of young people, many from the developing countries. The keynote speakers were to be Professor Bengt Jangfeldt, a member of the Academy of Sweden, an historian and Russian specialist, and Claudio Magris, Professor of German Literature at Trieste, an important writer and strongly anti-Fascist historian, with whom I felt a great affinity as his language when speaking about Nazi murders was closely akin to my intemperate outbursts. Professor Jangfeldt was to sketch in the history of the epoch, I was to be the survivor and person 'on the ground', while Magris was to outline moral conclusions to be drawn from such events.

On arrival in Rome I was picked up by the ambassador's car and taken to the Santa Brigida convent, an elegant yet humble converted monastery in the centre of Rome, adjacent to the French Embassy. Ambassadors and dignitaries of many nations use the convenient facilities of this convent, established by Swedish nuns about 200 years ago. The conference, a memorable event, took place in August 2012, under the chairmanship of the head of the Sant'Egidio community. Among those present were two heads of Papal Commissions, those for Interfaith Relations and for Peace and Justice, the head of the Jewish Community in Rome, and about a dozen ambassadors representing Western countries accredited to the Vatican.

Prior to the conference I had the opportunity to partake in interviews by various radio and television networks. I had an individual interview on Vatican Radio, which was relayed to many European countries. Spanish television conducted a separate interview, and the Hungarian news service asked me to discuss the concepts of forgiveness and forgetting, both of which were alien to my thinking, which I did not try to hide. In the event my comments appeared on numerous Catholic and Protestant websites in Hungary.

The seminar was attended by about 200 people. The Italian version of my speech, plus a modified English one, were printed in the Vatican weekly newspaper, *Osservatore Romano*. During the course of these events I was able to peruse some of the Vatican Museum's displays, accompanied by the Ambassador to the Holy Sea and a translator, so our journey through the displays passage was made easy. During a visit to the Jewish Museum, in which our guide was a surviving witness of the Holocaust in Rome, I was particularly taken by the attention to detail in preserving history, which in this case extended back over 2500 years to when the Jewish people first settled in Rome. Among the exhibits were exquisite embroideries from pre-Roman times and liturgical materials preserved in the original. One document I particularly remember was a Nazi warrant ordering inhabitants to leave their house and assemble outside immediately for 're-settlement', the famous euphemism for deportation. In fact, of the more than 4000 Jewish inhabitants of the ghetto in Rome who were deported within the space of 48 hours, the vast majority were gassed in Auschwitz.

At the Vatican Commission for Peace and Justice a lady spoke of problems facing the developing world. At the Commission of Interfaith relations a Vatican official spoke understandingly of the lessons of the Shoah, and I had the opportunity to mention Irene Sendler, a Polish lady who had saved over 2000 children from the Warsaw ghetto, transporting them under the nose of the Germans in her cart, with a savage dog growling to frighten them off. In spite of brutal torture she refused to reveal the names of her collaborators. She was bailed out by the Polish underground who bribed some prison officials to put off her execution, and she survived the war. She received the 'Righteous Gentile' title from Yad Vashem, but my efforts to get her recognition from the Vatican have been unsuccessful.

Since the conference Professor Bengt Jangfeldt has published his biography of Wallenberg – *The Hero of Budapest: The Triumph and Tragedy of Raoul Wallenberg* (2014) – based on the most recently available documents and illustrations obtained from various family, Swedish and other sources. He made great use of the Jenő Lévai's *Raoul Wallenberg regényes élete, hősi küzdelmei, rejtélyes eltűnésének titka* (*Raoul Wallenberg's Eventful Life, Heroic Struggles and the Secret of His Mysterious Disappearance*), which I had translated. Jangfeldt's sense of history made this book a riveting document. The latest book added to the considerable bibliography of the Raoul Wallenberg saga is Ingrid Carlberg's *Raoul Wallenberg – A Biography*, to be launched in 2016.

Claudio Magris is an attractive figure whose history of the course of the river Danube (*Danube: A Sentimental Journey from the Source to the Black Sea*) covers the geography of the lands surrounding it, as well as the myths, superstitions, customs and arts of adjacent populations. On the dark side, he devotes chapters to recent war crimes, including some of the most despicable figures in modern history such as Dr Mengele. His language in dealing with such scum is similar to what I would like to employ dealing with this depressing topic. Magris is an expert on German literature, but in his soul he is an Italian and a socialist. It was a great honour to have met him and Bengt Jangfeldt in the course of these events.

After the conference the family of Archbishop Verolino hosted a dinner and we have had numerous contacts with them since that time.

Chapter Fourteen

WALLENBERG'S HONORARY AUSTRALIAN CITIZENSHIP

The Road to the Citizenship

Honorary Citizenship is a rare and symbolic recognition of the service to humanity and to a nation that an individual has rendered in war or peace. It is very much an award depending on the approval by the head of state, the government and the parliament. Raoul Wallenberg was accorded this honour by the United States in 1981, where President Reagan stated that 'when we honour Wallenberg we honour ourselves', and by Canada in 1985. Israel made Wallenberg an Honorary Citizen in 1986, and he has also been made an Honorary Citizen of Budapest (2003), but not of Hungary.

I wrote a letter to the Australian Ministry of Immigration and Citizenship in 1983 asking for this matter to be considered, but it was countered by a low-level response pointing out that no precedent existed. This was an indication of the bureaucratic framework we faced. Subsequently Wallenberg's name became widely known in Australia and recognition was granted via, for example, a stamp being issued in his honour. This was achieved after a commercial deal with Australia Post for a limited issue, organised by the B'nai B'rith. They also tried to lobby the government in more recent years, as did the Sydney Wallenberg Committee.

At the time of the centenary tribute for Raoul Wallenberg, in 2012, I contacted leading members of the Australian community, headed by the Governor of Victoria, and the question of honorary citizenship was mentioned, especially as representatives of countries who had named Wallenberg an Honorary Citizen attended the ceremony and paid tribute. The flags of nations who were concerned with Wallenberg's deeds were displayed on this occasion.

Some weeks later, the Minister for Foreign Affairs, Bob Carr, spoke of Wallenberg in Canberra at a tree planting ceremony, delivering a well-researched and moving oration. I had not been able to attend the Canberra ceremony, but following it I wrote to Carr as Minister. I referred to the many distinguished members of Australian society who supported the move towards Honorary Citizenship for Wallenberg. These dignitaries included the Governor General, H.E. Quentin Bryce AC, who sent a gracious message to the tribute ceremony, at which messages were also received from the then Prime Minister Julia Gillard and Leader of the Opposition Tony Abbott. These were all read at the dinner hosted by the B'nai B'rith. Influential members of both sides of the political spectrum, including the then Attorney General, Mark Dreyfus, and the Liberal MP Josh Frydenberg, had previously spoken of Wallenberg in Parliament and at public meetings, which ensured bipartisan support. A comment in *The Age* newspaper, on the granting of this honorary award, is worth recording: 'We can imagine the battle Mark Dreyfus had to wage to gain acceptance by the public service of the fact that Parliament is in charge and not Sir Humphrey Appleby.'

From here, I think the words and documents of the individuals involved speak most powerfully of Raoul Wallenberg's enduring legacy, and capacity to unite people, even across political divides, in a common respect for and reverence towards humanity.

Address on Raoul Wallenberg given by Senator Bob Carr, Minister for Foreign Affairs, at the Australian National University, 26 November, 2012

May I begin with some words about Raoul Wallenberg from a Melbourne citizen, Professor Frank Vajda: 'I owe a debt to this man. I owe my life to this man. I owe my mother's life to this man. I honour him. How can you honour him other than by making people think, ask questions and remember.' Dr Vajda and his mother Maria had been among the many thousand Hungarian Jews saved by Raoul Wallenberg and the Swedish rescue operation in Budapest in the last months of 1944 and early 1945. They had been issued with one of his famous fake passports in October 1944. In the words I just quoted, Dr Vajda was explaining his part in establishing Australia's first memorial to Raoul Wallenberg. It's in Studley Park Road and Denmark Road, Melbourne. A garden was dedicated by the Kew City Council in 1982, and a monument was erected there in 1985. The Melbourne memorial has the proud distinction of having been the first memorial to Raoul

Wallenberg outside Budapest. The second Australian memorial is at Edgecliff Road and Queen Street Woollahra, Sydney. The memorial garden was dedicated also in 1985. Then, in March 1989, the Prime Minister, Bob Hawke, named a tree in Raoul Wallenberg's honour, in front of the new Parliament House. 1989 is a landmark year for Europe and the world and for the Wallenberg story. It was only then, with the collapse of the Warsaw Pact, and the glasnost period in the Soviet Union, that we began to learn something of the truth about his disappearance in January 1945.

In June 1989, Prime Minister Hawke laid a wreath at the memorial to Raoul Wallenberg in Budapest. It had just been restored. In 1949, forty years before, the regime had dismantled the monument, in the dead of night, on the very eve of its unveiling. Now, in the nation's capital, we come to dedicate this memorial, marking the hundredth year since Raoul Wallenberg's birth. I am deeply grateful to the Ambassadors of Hungary, Israel and Sweden. Our presence here today results from their joint initiative and invitation. We come to remember and honour Raoul Wallenberg's courage and sacrifice. In the words of the mission statement of the Wallenberg Committee of the United States 'to remind the world that the heroic actions of a single person have the power to make a difference'. We remember and honour his fellow Swedes from the legation, and the Red Cross, and the many Hungarians who risked everything to help them. Let us remember and honour, too, the ten thousand men and women across Europe identified by the Yad Vashem Memorial in Jerusalem as 'the righteous among the nations'.

And in all these acts of remembrance, a special duty rests heavily upon us. It's there in the words I quoted at the beginning: 'The duty to think and ask questions'. For Australians there's a question which goes to the very meaning of our existence as a nation of immigrants. In July 1938, on the urging of President Roosevelt, the representatives of 32 nations including Australia, convened at Evian on the French Riviera, to discuss the plight of the Jewish refugees, now desperately worsened by the Anschluss, incorporating Austria into the Third Reich. The utterly negative outcome of the Evian Conference was pre-determined. The invitation to the Conference stated that 'no country would be expected to receive a greater number of emigrants than is permitted by its existing legislation'. This was the cue for the Australian representative to assert that 'Australia had no racial problems and didn't wish to import one'.

All the more reprehensible, that this proposition should be put forward in Australia's name, in the light of our own highly positive Jewish experience. In 1931, the commander-in-chief of the First A.I.F. in France, Sir John Monash, was buried with Jewish rites in Melbourne after the largest funeral ever held in Australia. A quarter of a million people, as many as a third of them ex-servicemen, lined the processional route. In 1936, Sir Isaac Isaacs had completed his term as the first Australian-born Governor-General. Before that, he had been Chief Justice of the High Court of Australia. Australia's biggest department store proudly proclaimed the name of its founder – Sidney Myer. The Australian comic genius, Roy Rene, was at the height of its popularity. Such was the standing of the Australian Jewish community in 1938. The official stance at Evian demeaned Australia. It was not even a legitimate expression of the egregious White Australia Policy. I cannot help but reflect, with infinite sadness, what a difference Australia could have made at that time. And what a difference, in terms of the enrichment of our national life, if we had stood up and welcomed 20,000 or 40,000 German and Austrian Jewish refugees.

Before the war, before the holocaust, the most sinister aspect of Evian was the reaction in Berlin. The SD – the Security Section of the SS – reported on the Conference. The report singled out Australia as an example of the hypocrisy of the democracies: 'It was remarkable' the SD report said 'that the Australian delegate even maintained that Jewish emigration would endanger his own race'. And Hitler himself used the Evian fiasco to taunt the democracies in a speech at the Reichstag in September 1938 – two weeks before Munich and two months before Kristallnacht. The Head of the Jewish Section of the SD in 1938 was Adolf Eichmann. Six years later, Eichmann went to Budapest to plan and supervise the destruction of the Hungarian Jews. That was what brought Wallenberg to Budapest. He volunteered to join the Swedish legation in Budapest to do what he could to thwart Eichmann's scheme to accelerate and complete the extermination of the Jews of Europe. To this end, he pulled out every stop and broke every rule. The distinguished Swedish diplomat Per Anger who was secretary of the Swedish legation with Wallenberg, has left this description of his style: Wallenberg was a talented actor which was a big help in his clashes with the Nazis. He could be calm, humorous and warm, or aggressive and intimidating. He could flatter and bribe on occasion, and shout and threaten on another. The Nazis were impressed.

The last time Per Anger saw Wallenberg was 10 January 1945. Per Anger urged Wallenberg to seek safety. Raoul Wallenberg replied: 'To me there's no other choice. I've accepted this assignment and I could not return to Stockholm without the knowledge that I'd done everything in human power to save as many Jews as possible'. One week later, Raoul Wallenberg contacted the advancing Soviet army and was arrested. A victim it would seem, of the suspicion and ill-will that was already developing between the West and the Soviet Union. He is thought to have perished in the Gulag in July 1947.

In one sense, we may see Raoul Wallenberg, who had done so much to save others, as an early casualty of the Cold War. So tremendous and terrible tides of history bring us here today to honour, to remember, and, I trust, to continue to ask questions which go to the heart of the human condition. It is wholly fitting that the memorial should be placed at the Australian National University and near the School for European Studies. It connects us symbolically with events of commanding importance to Europe, Australia and the world – in the 20th century, and in the 21st century. Here, truly, in these peaceful surroundings, we can remember – and learn.

Letter, 3 December, 2012, from Professor Frank Vajda to Hon. Senator Bob Carr

Dear Minister,

I wish to thank you most sincerely for your gracious remarks in your introductory paragraphs at the Canberra tribute for Raoul Wallenberg, when you quoted me and made reference to Raoul Wallenberg saving my life. Your speech was profoundly moving and showed a clear reflection of your research, understanding and good will in relation to this great humanitarian and his deeds. You had referred to Australia's pre-eminence role in the fight for Wallenberg's release and to the statue of Wallenberg in Melbourne, the first statue outside of Hungary. Australia however lags behind other countries viz. Canada, Israel and the United States in granting Wallenberg honorary citizenship. I humbly ask you to use your evident good will, immense influence and enormous prestige to try to expedite this issue, namely granting Raoul Wallenberg honorary citizenship of Australia. I tried to ask for this move in 1984 but I was referred to an assistant of the relevant Ministry who fobbed me off in a three line letter. The situation has now altered and Raoul Wallenberg's stature as the most significant humanitarian of the Holocaust has been widely recognised in this country – and worldwide.

My request to you, Sir, carries the support of various Wallenberg-related organisations, the Jewish community, the Ambassadors who joined you on the 26th November, 2012 at the ANU in Canberra as well as many of your parliamentary colleagues, amongst them Mr Mark Dreyfus and Mr Josh Frydenberg, as well as very prominent Australians such as Professor Ed Byrne, Vice-Chancellor of Monash University, Richard Divall, Maestro of Australian Music, Jack Martin FRS and Sam Berkovic FRS. Australia's Governor General, the Hon. Quentin Bryce AC, the Prime Minister and the Leader of the Opposition both sent glowing messages relating the deeds of the Swedish Diplomat, and the Governor of Victoria, H.E. The Hon. Alex Chernov AC QC, personally attended the ceremony and acted as Guest of Honour for the Melbourne tribute.

With sincere good wishes,

Frank Vajda

Letter, 14 February, 2013, from Hon. Senator Bob Carr to Professor Frank Vajda

SENATOR THE HON BOB CARR

MINISTER FOR FOREIGN AFFAIRS
CANBERRA

Professor Frank Vajda AM
857 Glenferrie Rd
KEW VIC 3101

14 FEB 2013

Dear Professor Vajda

Thank you for your kind letter of December 3, 2012, regarding the possibility of honorary citizenship for Raoul Wallenberg.

It was my deep privilege to dedicate the garden at the Australian National University on November 26 in his memory. I felt it important to open my speech with your moving testimony about Mr Wallenberg, given the important role you have played in bringing his story to the attention of the Australian people.

I personally support your call to make Mr Wallenberg an honorary Australian citizen, and have brought this matter to the attention of the Prime Minister and other relevant Ministers. Careful consideration is currently being given to this idea, which would - if awarded - be the first ever occasion that an honorary Australian citizenship has been bestowed.

Thank you once again for your letter.

Yours sincerely

Bob Carr

Letter, 20 February, 2013, from Professor Frank Vajda to Hon. Senator Bob Carr

Professor Frank Vajda AM
Officer1st cl, Royal Order of the Polar Star (Sweden)
MD FRCP Ed FRACP
Neurologist, Neuropharmacologist

857 Glenferrie Road
Kew Vic 3101 Australia
Tel: (613) 98193056
email: vajda@netspace.net.au
Prov no. 242675Y

20.Feb.2013

The Hon Senator Bob Carr
Minister for Foreign Affairs
Canberra ACT 2600

Dear Minister,

Thank you most humbly for your wonderful letter and support.
I am proud to be an Australian!
With sincere good wishes,

Frank Vajda

Director, Australian Pregnancy Register
Department of Medicine and Neuroscience, University of Melbourne

Email, 15 April, 2013, from Mr Bruce Wolpe, Prime Minister's Office, to Professor Frank Vajda

Dear Prof Vajda,

Kind regards to you. Josh Frydenberg has referred me to you – a pretty significant announcement is below for your information. Can we talk by phone for a few minutes? I very much hope you and your wife might be able to attend in Canberra on May 6.

Thank you,

Bruce Wolpe,

Senior Advisor, Prime Minister Julia Gillard

[Forwarded message from the Prime Minister's Office]

Subject: Re: PRIME MINISTER – MEDIA RELEASE – HONORARY AUSTRALIAN CITIZENSHIP TO BE AWARDED TO RAOUL WALLENBERG – CANBERRA – 15 APRIL 2013

Email, 15 April, 2013, from Professor Frank Vajda to Bruce Wolpe

Dear Mr Wolpe,

Thank you very much for your message. I am overjoyed and very deeply gratified by the events. May I convey my deepest respects and appreciation to the Prime Minister and Senator Bob Carr, whose efforts culminated in this decision to award the Honorary Citizenship to Mr Raoul Wallenberg, the Hero of the Holocaust.

May I also thank most sincerely Mr Frydenberg for his support and all members of Parliament who supported the move. I would be more than happy to talk to you on the phone this afternoon.

Kindest regards,

Frank Vajda

Media release, 15 April, 2013, from Prime Minister Julia Gillard

Subject: PRIME MINISTER – MEDIA RELEASE – HONORARY AUSTRALIAN CITIZENSHIP TO BE AWARDED TO RAOUL WALLENBERG – CANBERRA – 15 APRIL 2013

I am pleased to announce that the late Raoul Wallenberg will be recognised as an honorary Australian citizen. This is the first time that Australia has bestowed such an honour. Raoul Wallenberg was a Swedish diplomat who led an extraordinary rescue operation in Hungary during World War II. He saved tens of thousands of Jews from the Holocaust by issuing protective passports and providing shelter in diplomatic buildings. Tragically, Raoul Wallenberg did not return to Sweden. He was arrested by Soviet troops in January 1945 and his fate remains a mystery. Mr Wallenberg has been recognised as an honorary citizen of the United States of America, Canada, Hungary and Israel. Many monuments, buildings, streets, schools and other institutions around the world bear his name. He was awarded the honour of 'Righteous among the Nations' by Yad Vashem, the Jewish people's living memorial to the Holocaust. The lives of those he rescued are Mr Wallenberg's greatest memorial and Australia is honoured to have survivors he rescued living in Australia today.

The Governor-General, Her Excellency Ms Quentin Bryce AC CVO, will host the presentation of a certificate of honorary Australian citizenship at Government House, Canberra, on Monday, 6 May 2013. The award is made in the year of the centenary of Mr Wallenberg's birth. The award of honorary Australian citizenship is symbolic recognition of Mr Wallenberg's tireless devotion to human life during the Holocaust. The award is not conferred under the Citizenship Act 2007.

The Governor General's speech, from the Canberra Press Office, 15 April 2013

The Governor-General, Ms Quentin Bryce AC CVO, presided at a ceremony at Government House, Canberra, recognising the late humanitarian Raoul Wallenberg – a Swedish diplomat in Nazi-occupied Hungary who led a mission to save the lives of nearly 100,000 Hungarian Jews, as the first honorary Australian citizen. The following is an edited version of the Governor General's address to Holocaust survivors and others who benefited involved because of Wallenberg's courage.

'The Nobel laureate, writer and Holocaust survivor Elie Wiesel has said: "The opposite of love is not hate, it's indifference. The opposite of art is not ugliness, it's indifference. The opposite of faith is not heresy, it's indifference. And the opposite of life is not death, it's indifference." With these words, Professor Wiesel has reminded the world of its tragic failure to prevent one of the darkest periods in human history, the Holocaust.

'In Australia Wallenberg has already been honoured by parks and monuments created in his name. I am proud that today our nation goes one step further in making Raoul Wallenberg our first ever honorary citizen. I cannot think of a more appropriate and significant figure to welcome to our Australian family. Wallenberg's life is an example to us all. His brave, selfless and compassionate actions are proof that just one person can make a real difference.

'Today may not have occurred but for the efforts of people who understand how important it is to perpetuate Raoul Wallenberg's memory. None more so than Dr Frank Vajda, who, with his mother Maria, were rescued by Wallenberg. You have done so much to honour his name. To you we say thank you.'

REFLECTIONS

Since submission of the manuscript for publication, Raoul Wallenberg has been honoured further in Australia. A stamp, bearing his portrait, a *Schutzpass* and his name, was issued by Australia Post in a series of postage stamps and first day covers commemorating Wallenberg, together with Nelson Mandela and Sister Theresa. I would like to thank Mrs J. Schiff for her efforts in bringing this to fruition.

An exhibition created by the Swedish Foreign Office opened in Adelaide in October 2015 in the State Library, attended by the Hon Hieu Van Le AO, Governor of South Australia, and the Swedish Ambassador H.E. Par Ahlberger. I was invited to speak of my recollections of Wallenberg. The exhibition is scheduled to tour the country in 2016.

In October 2015, Raoul Wallenberg's Trustee in Sweden, at the request of Raoul's family, issued a declaration of death, thus ending the period of lingering uncertainty about his possible return. He would have been 103 this year.

In September 2015 I was invited to Istanbul to receive the International Award of Ambassador for Epilepsy, and the citation stressed the role of Raoul Wallenberg in my survival and motivation.

The quest for discovering the truth about Wallenberg's fate goes on. A symposium of interested parties is planned to be held in a European capital, not yet specified, in order to discuss outstanding issues and leads. This symposium will compromise leading figures involved from many countries, including Sweden, and all continents.

Although we have to accept the sad fact that Raoul Wallenberg will never return physically to those who hold him dear, his deeds and persona will forever be etched in the hearts of those he saved, their families, descendants and their large circle of friends and colleagues, and in the hearts of the many people across the globe who value compassion, courage and humanity.

APPENDIX ONE: DEPOSITIONS

Deposition 1

This document relates to events leading up to the incident when 36 Jewish inmates were taken away from the Alice Weiss hospital by Arrow Cross militia, an incident described in the section 'The Last Escape' in chapter three, 'Eight Close Shaves'. This is my translation of the 1946 deposition by the director of the Hospital to the Committee for the Care of the Deportees.

Name: M.T., Dr., male
Profession: Director/Chief Physician, Alice Weiss Maternity
                   Hospital Budapest

The above named M.T. wishes to state the following:

At the beginning of the German era, already in the first days of April, 1944, the Germans appeared at the Alice Weiss hospital and wanted to acquire it. A few days later a similar group arrived with an identical purpose. The first group wished to take over the hospital for the SS and the second wanted it for the Luftwaffe. I managed to play off one group against the other, by saying that the other group had already acquired it, and vice versa.

In about June, another group of Germans appeared. This took place at the time when they had requisitioned our neighbour, the Jewish Hospital. Again they wished to take over ours as well. I managed to find an approach to the officer who was charged with providing an opinion about the hospital. Quite simply, by using bribery I was able to achieve that he gave a report that the hospital had no adequate air raid shelter, and therefore it was not suitable for the purpose of being a German military hospital. After this episode we enjoyed a period of calm and the German-related problems have ceased, at least for the time being. Our hospital was able getting involved with the process of rescuing certain people from the internment camps, under the guise of giving them medical treatment, and accommodating them in the hospital, in large numbers.

From the point of view of bombing raids, our hospital was in a very grave and dangerous situation. By virtue of its location, it was in the centre of the area targeted by Allied bombing. The Allies knew that there was a railway centre close-by, as well as a military food supply store, the German military hospital, (the former Jewish Hospital), and a railway station at Rákosrendezö etc. We have been subjected to the most frightful bombing raids. In August the Germans once again visited the hospital. This time they turned up with the accusation that that they received information about a secret radio transmitter station. Naturally they found nothing, and fortunately we managed to get over this visit as well without any consequences. *[There was a receiver for BBC broadcasts, which my mother was listening to.]*

In October, immediately after the proclamation by Regent Horthy the following day Arrow Cross soldiers walked into the hospital and carried off 16 employees, clerks and nurses and on the pretext that they have not worn their yellow star inside the hospital. We found out later that that one of the employees of the hospital denounced us. Those selected were taken to the neighbouring Albrecht military barracks, where they were very brutally treated threatened with machine guns and that they would be lined up in front of them. By chance there happened to be a more humane general, who liberated them and let them go. *[The 'humane general' was Wallenberg.]* Afterwards, however, the Arrow Cross turned up again to check everybody's documents.

In October we adapted our maternity hospital to adjust caring for males as well as females. Innumerable suicide cases, beaten, wounded Jews were brought in, men and women alike. Later those who escaped from the banks of the Danube were brought in, amongst them two young boys, one of whom unfortunately died soon after arrival because of his injuries. On the 6th December there was another raid. This time the raiders said that they had been sent to check whether there were any in the hospital, who were not really ill. This time we were lucky, everybody was left unharmed.

As we found out, the same day, they have taken a lot of people away from other institutions to place them in the ghetto. The next day – at night in fact – we were visited by another three Arrow Cross men, who came by car. They were searching for two Jewish women, but fortunately they did not find them. Had they found them with us, we would have had terrible trouble as a result.

On January 2nd, the hospital boilers got struck by a bomb. The laundry staff were washing in the laundry and thick smoke appeared to rise from the chimney. The next morning some soldiers appeared, amongst them a man dressed as a German soldier. They went straight to the laundry. They declared that they discovered why so many bombs have hit the area: "the Jews have been sending smoke signals!" They promised that they would send a patrol to apprehend us. The next day, at half past 11, on the January 3rd, about 20 Arrow Cross men appeared. They came past the fence and jumped over the gate. By this time we had night watchmen placed around the hospital. They noticed Arrow Cross men sneaking around, and reported this to the doctor on duty. Very soon they started banging on the big inside gate.

An Aryan nurse led them in. They came down to the basement and demanded that everybody should present their documents. They threatened to take away everybody, except those who could prove they were Aryans, pregnant women in the last stages of pregnancy, suckling mothers and those above the age of 75. Aryans were segregated, but they wanted to take even those who were in mixed marriages, and they said they would let them go after checking their documents.

They handed me a service-warrant which read as follows:

> We received denunciations against Dr. M.T., Chief Physician/Director of the Alice Weiss Hospital, that he is hiding several hundred Jews in the cellars and lofts of the hospital. The Jews are living there under the ruse of being sick, but there is nothing wrong with them. They are in constant touch with the world outside through an organisation called 'Villam' [Lightning]. Amongst those hiding there are Henrik Biró and Armin Spiegel. We demand the strictest action.

I made the men who brought this service warrant sit down. They questioned me for an hour and a half. This conversation was relatively friendly and courteous, but during questioning they felt it was necessary to comment that they preferred that ten innocent Jews should perish, rather than one guilty one escape unharmed. They examined all the documents, medical and exemption certificates, and medical histories. I showed them the regulation, which applied to us as a public hospital, according to which we were forbidden to accept anyone for admission unless they were gravely ill. I repeatedly offered my personal guarantee, but only if a committee comprised of experts examines all the patients. They asked who was on the committee and who were the people specified in the regulation? I hastened to add that they were totally reliable, as the regulation has only recently been authorised.

The Arrow Cross men replied that that they do not believe me as they have been deceived many times. As I mentioned, this discussion took about one and a half hours. One or two of them seemed already inclined to agree not to take anyone, another however declared that they will take away some people, but only to their headquarters, and they will check their documents there, and bring them back immediately. They chose 36 people. This was carried out by going through the hospital, and asking who was who and what their ages were.

They asked one of the patients what was the matter with him. He said he was a diabetic. They ordered him to show the sites of insulin injections. This examination was fortunate as the person was really receiving injections of insulin. The selection was totally arbitrary. We had three doctors, Professor Lajos Török, Dr. István Vágó, a senior physician, and Dr. Henrik Biró, a surgeon general. They asked Dr. Török his age. He was 81 and so he was allowed to stay. Then came Dr. Vágó. He replied to the question whether he was a doctor or a patient saying he was there as a patient, so he was made to join the ranks of those ready to be taken. The third man was Dr. Henrik Biró, a surgeon-general, and although he was 84, he was taken, the Arrow Cross saying that he would be taken even if he had been a field marshal.

We smuggled out of the group whomever we could, at the end the Arrow Cross got fed up with this and threatened us that if we did not stop this practice, they would take everybody. Thirty six people got included in the group to be dragged off, of whom one patient, Elizabeth Rajna, was able to escape from the road leading to the Danube and return to the hospital. *[Elizabeth Rajna's survival is described in the next document.]* That night we had some more excitement at dawn: yelling and mad panic broke the silence of the hospital. It turned out that a worker who wanted to fill up a kerosene lamp dropped it in his anxiety, and the canister blew up.

This deposition confirms our encounter with the Gestapo, our brutal removal to the Albrecht barracks, our rescue by the 'humane general' (Wallenberg), and the return the same day by the Arrow Cross, who took away a large group of people for 'documentation'.

Deposition 2

This is the official deposition, in my translation, of the sole survivor of those taken away, Elizabeth Rajna, given to the Committee for the Care of Returning Deportees after Liberation, and confirmed in a radio interview forty years later by the person giving the deposition.

Name: Mrs. E.R.
Female
Born in Budapest, 1920, office worker

The above named wishes to state the following:

I have spent the period of the siege of Budapest in the Alice Weiss Hospital. On the night of 2 January 1945 a group of Arrow Cross entered the gates of the Hospital, in order to "check the *Schutzpasses*" – according to their statement. Naturally they did not find them to be order and so they continued "checking the documentations".

They collected us in a large room and chose us, 36 people, to stand apart. Amongst those selected there was one person over the age of 70, but there were some who were very ill, eg. people suffering from cancer. I asked for permission to go up to my room to collect my belongings, but this was granted only under an escort. On the pretext that they are going to check our papers – as I later found out at 3.00 am – they dragged us away, under intense shelling and aerial bombardment. They took us to the Arrow Cross house on Pozsonyi road. First they made us go into a totally dark room, and later in order to check documentation they took us to another room, where the "checking committee" under the pretext of checking, took away almost all of our belongings. They took my overcoat, gloves, my watch, they turned my pockets inside out, they made me take off the two blouses I was wearing and checked if I had hidden anything, and if there were any valuables sewn into the lining of clothes. In the end they even took my handkerchief.

After the search we were all sent to the entrance hall, and after we were all gathered together, they went to check if we left any food or valuables in the room where we were searched. Of course if they found anything at all, they took it. After this they made us go back to the room where we were kept originally. A few people were there already, so that when our group of 36 arrived, we may have been about 42 persons. We tried to get comfortable, as best we could. The Arrow Cross man in charge took great care to ensure we did not speak to each other. We got nothing to eat, but if we wanted water,

Appendix One: Depositions

then very reluctantly they gave us some. I must note that at the Alice Weiss hospital we were ignorant of the outside world, and the stories of being marched to the banks of the Danube – which by then was a regular daily occurrence – have not reached us, so I suspected nothing, and thought that they would rob us and then escort us to the ghetto. In the morning one of us enquired: "what is to become of us, where are they taking us?" The answer was: "to Buda, to work". All day long we sat there, downcast, exhausted from fatigue, finally at night they lined us up, to form pairs and marched us off.

It was a clear, bright night, we could clearly see the ongoing battle. Without a coat, poorly dressed we were freezing cold. Our march took us towards Parliament, on the Pest side. We had a terrible scene facing us, over the whole of the Danube embankment there were corpses and dead horses. We arrived to the Chain Bridge. They wanted us to descend on the steps next to the Parliament. My neighbour then remarked at this point: "Listen, they are planning something evil!"

By then the stairs were damaged by the bombing, it was impossible to descend along them to the riverbank. The Arrow Cross leader then informed us that we are going to cross to the Buda side of the Danube. We crossed along the Chain Bridge, and after crossing our direction was towards the Margaret Bridge. They ordered us to the lower embankment. Women walked in front, followed the men. There were about eight men. Suddenly the leader said: "The men to fall behind!" and we, the women went on.

Then we heard several rifle shots close by. My neighbour again remarked: "They shot them!"

I could still not believe that they were so evil and I remarked to her that one could not shoot at so many people without any sound being heard. I did not know yet at that time what it means if somebody is shot from close range into the back of the head. We were ordered to turn around. By then I became certain that they wanted nothing else but to murder us, because if they had any other intentions they would have taken us further. I cannot say that I was afraid, I was rather surprised, I could not grasp that everything was finished. The others were also quiet. They told us to line up one by one, facing the river.

A 15-year-old little girl stood next to me with her mother and her aunt; it only occurred to her to shout for help, and yell in her thin childish voice. They started to shoot down these poor people, one by one. I did not know what to do, my instincts told me the best thing would be to throw myself on the ground. I cannot account for how this thought came to me, I could not explain now, maybe I wanted to die this way. My poor neighbour, who came to the hospital originally after attempting suicide and wanted to die at all costs, started yelling after the shots were aimed at her, that she was still alive. I heard the voice of one of the Arrow Cross who asked who it was who had yelled, and afterwards shot her again. I decided not to make a move, they will either shoot me and then it is all over in a second, or I carry this through. They checked if I was moving and I heard as they commented: "This one is dead already!" They did not shoot me again, but the lady next to me was shot again.

It was a moonlit night, and besides the water carried the sounds very well, and thus I saw and heard everything very clearly. I knew that the next step would be to throw the bodies into the Danube. I resolved to pretend I was dead. I saw through half closed eyes that they began hauling the corpses one after the other towards the water and I felt an Arrow Cross man grabbed me by the legs and dragged me away. I must note that this part of the riverbank is a steep tall wall, there are no steps here. I felt as he dragged me to the wall, my upper body fell and then he let my leg go. Even here I was fortunate in that the distance of the fall was reduced by the length of my body and so I fell a shorter distance. I felt I was falling, the Arrow Cross let my leg go, but I did not fall into the water, but landed between the water and the wall, at a distance of one and a half meters. I took care not to move. I fell on my face, I did not even notice the impact, and noted later that I fell on soft sand. I remained motionless. The water level was shallow; the river did not take the bodies of my poor murdered companions immediately. I heard as they remarked on top of the wall: "The water will carry them away," I heard this comment quite distinctly, and I observed everything very closely. The voices became ever fainter, as they left the scene.

I lifted my head carefully and looked up. Behind me a soft voice said: "Do not move, they are still here!" My companion was able to look up on the wall. I waited for I do not know how long, half an hour, maybe two hours? I worked out that they would have gone, I tried to get up very carefully. I did not know what had happened, whether I could stand up, was I alive? I was not sure about the situation, I started to touch myself. I was able to stand, and suffered no physical damage, only my nose bled a little, I injured it when I fell on my face, it was quite an insignificant abrasion. I looked around trying to get my bearings, I felt as though I was dreaming. The lady who spoke earlier spoke again: "I am the sister of the Matron, if you survive and you are able to summon help, call the police or an ambulance!" I knew this was in vain, as the ambulances by this time were not functioning. I started

Appendix One: Depositions

yelling with a full blast: "Help! Police! Ambulance!" I heard nothing, only the wailing from the direction of the shot men, and the screeching sound of the ice on the river.

Nobody was coming this way. I was desolate to realise that shouting was quite useless. In front of me there was the fast moving river, I had no clothes in the freezing January winter, behind me the steep wall of the embankment, no steps, and all around me the corpses. Russian artillery shells were raining from Pest to Buda. I tried to assist the poor dying lady, I hauled her out towards the bank, she was frightfully heavy, I did not know what I could do for her. I tried to orientate myself about who were those people who were shot by the murderers. I saw a lady still breathing, I pulled her out of the water. I started thinking: it is unwise to stay here, I must get away as quickly as possible. In the distance I saw a military pontoon type bridge; I thought I must reach this at all costs. With my snow boots still with me I tried to wade into the river, in order to reach that bridge. The water was deep; I failed. By then my survival instinct was roused and by now I wanted to survive at all costs.

I went back to the edge of the sand bank, but not to the corpses, rather but a little distance further. I sat on the ground and waited. A little later I saw about 7 to 8 German soldiers cross the bridge, get into a wide naval boat, rowing and by chance start rowing directly in my direction. Their leader noticed me and remarked: "Da ist jemand!" ["Someone is there!"] Soon they reached me and landed. They thought I fell off the wall, and their leader asked me: "Hat weh getan?" ["Are you hurt?"] I promptly took stock of this and replied immediately: "Yes!" They got out of the boat, and standing on each others' shoulders climbed up to the wall, like walking up steps. I asked if they could help me get up as well.

The leader laughed and said: "Denken Sie nicht dass Sie sind ein bischen schwach?" ["Do you not think you are bit weak?"] I enquired if we could find an ambulance, he replied: "Nein, da sind schon die Russen!" ["No, the Russians are already here!"] He offered however that they take me in the boat, and take me to the riverbank, it is going to be 7 am very soon, and by then one was permitted to walk in the streets. He noted that that I was surprised at this as I had no idea of curfews, and that 7 am was the time for lifting the curfew. They encouraged me that although I could not get an ambulance, I was sure to find a policeman. They lifted me into the boat, covered me with a blanket, then landed at the military bridge; the leader escorted me to the shore. In fact I did not feel too bad, but pretended to be very ill. After a few steps it occurred to me to thank them for their help and offered to return the blanket. The leader told me to keep it. I started walking, but now faced a great problem, where to go? I did not know what to do. First I thought I would go to one of my Aryan friends living in Buda, but I did not wish to cause her any problems, and in any case my mother was at the Alice Weiss Hospital, and I wanted to get back to her at all costs. I was totally uniformed about how I could walk across the bridge without showing documentation. I walked along the lower embankment and did not encounter anybody.

At the Chain Bridge however I had to go up to the bridge. Only some soldiers were wandering about, no one took any notice of me, I did not appear to be unusual at all. They probably thought I was running to one of the air raid shelters. On the bridge I ran into a three man military patrol, and before they could have asked me anything I enquired if there was an ambulance station on the Pest side of the bridge, as I was wounded. I was lucky again as one of the more friendly looking soldiers replied that there was no ambulance station, but he did not think I was too badly wounded on my face, only slightly dirty. I should go towards the Elizabeth Bridge, where there was indeed an ambulance station. I could not but accept his advice and go that way. En route a soldier started to become suspicious and he stood in my way and in reply to my question how I can get across the Elizabeth Bridge he asked me why I need to get across at all, what am I doing here, anyway? I visited a girlfriend, I said. He asked me what I was doing, where does she live? "In Chain Bridge Street" I replied. He kept questioning me:

"Where is that? Where do you live?"

I named Damjanich Street, the address of our old flat. He then wanted to know how I intended get from the Elizabeth Bridge to Damjanich Street? After I outlined the route he quietened down, and said at this time the bridges were not under attack, and one may get across. After that I asked no more questions of anyone. I ran across the bridge, trying to avoid the Arrow Cross patrols. The scene in Kossuth Lajos Street was sheer devastation, but finally I reached the Alice Weiss Hospital.

This document sets out in detail the terrible fate we had escaped by virtue of Mother's instant reaction to disobey the order the Arrow Cross to present our documents for inspection. By this time we had been conditioned by our previous experience with 'documentation', when we were rescued in the last minute at the Albrecht Barracks, after being accused – correctly – of having removed the star of David.

APPENDIX TWO:
FREE WALLENBERG LETTER, C. 1984

FREE WALLENBERG

Patron: Sir Zelman Cowen, A.K., G.C.M.G., G.C.V.O., Q.C.

Chairman: Dr. Frank Vajda
Secretary: Dr. John Copland

Australian Committee:
815 Rathdowne Street,
Carlton, Victoria
Australia 3054
Telephone: (03) 380 2839
           (03) 783 7441

Sponsors
Phillip Adams
Senator the Hon. Donald Chipp
Emeritus Professor C. M. H. Clark, A.C.
Senator the Hon. Gareth Evans, Q.C.
Mina Fink, M.B.E.
Rt. Hon. Malcolm Fraser, C.H.
Max Harris
Hon. Robert J. L. Hawke, C.H., M.P.
Hon. Walter Jona
Hon. Barry Jones, M.P.
Thomas Keneally, F.R.S.L.
Dame Leonie Kramer, D.B.E.
Rabbi John Levi, A.M.
Stephen Murray-Smith, A.M.
Hon. Andrew Peacock, M.P.
Most Revd. David Penman,
   Archbishop of Melbourne
Morris L. West, A.M.
David Williamson, A.O.
Sir Douglas Wright, A.K.

We are writing to you on behalf of the Raoul Wallenberg Committee, sponsored by the leading personalities in public life named above, to focus your interest on the tragic case of Raoul Wallenberg and to ask your help in taking further action.

Wallenberg, in his capacity as a Swedish diplomat, saved tens of thousands of intended Hungarian victims from the Nazi gas chambers, by issuing Swedish protective passes, setting up protected houses and ignoring threats of retribution, and fearlessly opposing plans for deportation and mass murder.

His rescue mission has formed the subject of numerous books and films, and a summary is given in the enclosed pamphlet, based on John Bierman's "The Righteous Gentile".

At the end of the War Wallenberg was arrested in Budapest by the Russians and disappeared. There are persuasive reasons based on recent evidence, that he may still be alive.

We are conducting an appeal intended to raise $25,000 for three purposes; to support and develop activities to keep the Wallenberg issue alive and secure his release, or at least a satisfactory accounting for his fate; to institute an award within Australia for those who have worked unselfishly to relieve the suffering of others; to finance the sculpture of Raoul Wallenberg to be placed in the Raoul Wallenberg Garden in Kew, Victoria.

Wallenberg was not the only hero of the Holocaust, but in terms of the saving of lives he was outstandingly the most successful. Perhaps as important is the example he has shown us all that evil, against all odds can and must be opposed.

We most sincerely ask for your financial support for this most significant cause.

Yours sincerely,

Frank Vajda

APPENDIX THREE:
PER ANGER LETTER, 1999

Stockholm, April 23, 1999

Professor F.J.E. Vajda
Director
Australian Centre for Clinical Neuropharmacology
University Melbourne
St. Vincent's Hospital
Victoria Parade, Fitzroy Vic. 3065
Australia

Dear Professor Vajda,

Having learnt about your proposal to create a Raoul Wallenberg Institute of Neurosciences in Melbourne, it gives me great pleasure to support this project whole-heartedly.

This project is, in fact, very close to my heart, because it will tell the world about the unique deeds of Raoul Wallenberg during the Holocaust in Budapest, saving tens of thousands of Jews. It was my privilege to work with him and be part of this extraordinary mission.

I cannot but mention my admiration for your commitment to the cause of Raoul Wallenberg, and I wish you success in your efforts for the planned Institute.

Sincerely yours

Per Anger
Ambassador to Australia 1970-1975

ABOUT THE AUTHOR

Frank Vajda AM, Officer 1st.cl. Royal Order of Polar Star (Sweden), MD FRCP FRACP, is a consultant neurologist, Professorial Fellow, University of Melbourne, Director of the Australian Pregnancy Register of Antiepileptic Drugs, Past President of Epilepsy Society of Australia, International Ambassador for Epilepsy, Member of the International Pregnancy Register Board, Head of the Free Wallenberg Australian Committee and Founder of Raoul Wallenberg Centre of Clinical Neuropharmacology.